Scott Eyman / Paul Duncan (Ed.)

JOHN FORD

The Searcher 1894–1973

KÖLN LONDON LOS ANGELES MADRID PARIS TOKYO

FRONT COVER
Still from 'My Darling Clementine' (1946)
Wyatt Earp (Henry Fonda) in Monument Valley.

FIRST PAGE
Still from 'The Horse Soldiers' (1959)
John Wayne.

FRONTISPIECE
On the set of 'The Searchers' (1956)
John Ford shows Jeffrey Hunter the right way to kiss Vera Miles.

THIS PAGE
On the set of 'The Horse Soldiers' (1959)
Film stars John Wayne and William Holden are bemused as John Ford gets all the attention from admiring fans.

OPPOSITE
On the set of 'Cheyenne Autumn' (1964)
John Ford in Monument Valley, the mythical place where he shot several of his most important Westerns, like 'Stagecoach', 'My Darling Clementine' and 'The Searchers'.

BACK COVER
On the set of 'Cheyenne Autumn' (1964)
John Ford.

To stay informed about upcoming TASCHEN titles, please request our magazine at www.taschen.com or write to TASCHEN America, 6671 Sunset Boulevard, Suite 1508, Los Angeles, CA 90028, USA, Fax: +1-323-463.4442. We will be happy to send you a free copy of our magazine which is filled with information about all of our books.

© 2004 TASCHEN GmbH
Hohenzollernring 53, D–50672 Köln
www.taschen.com
Editor/Layout: Paul Duncan/Wordsmith Solutions
Editorial Coordination: Thierry Nebois, Cologne
Production Coordination: Ute Wachendorf, Cologne
Typeface Design: Sense/Net, Andy Disl, Cologne

Printed in Italy
ISBN 3-8228-3093-3

Thanks
To Dan Ford for paving the way with his book 'Pappy: The Life of John Ford' and for helping with this volume.

Images
British Film Institute Stills, Posters and Designs, London: 12/13, 14 (6), 15 (3), 16 (5), 17 (5), 26 (3), 27, 35top, 36bottom, 37t, 39top left +top right, 40, 43t, 44t+bl, 45, 46 (2), 47t, 51, 56 (2), 57 (2), 58t, 61t, 64b, 65 (2), 66 (2), 67, 70, 71 (2), 72, 72/73, 74t, 75, 84b, 89, 92t, 95, 96/97, 99 (2), 100i, 105, 114/115, 118, 124 (2), 139t, 144/145, 146, 149, 151, 155, 156/157, 160/161, 168t
Scott Eyman Collection, West Palm Beach: Front Cover, 2, 4, 14, 15 (3), 16, 17 (4), 18, 20, 21 (2), 24 (2), 28/29, 35b, 50, 54/55, 55, 60, 102/103, 106/107, 109, 120/121, 129, 134b, 137tl, 147 (2), 158, 162bl, 170l, 177, 180l
The Kobal Collection, London/New York: 6, 16, 17, 30t, 31b, 32 (2), 61b, 85, 87, 108 (2), 110, 134t, 137b, 142, 156, 167, 168b, 171, 187, 190b
L. Tom Perry Special Collections, Harold B. Lee Library, Brigham Young University, Provo, Utah: 132/133, 140, 141
Springer/Photofest, New York: 192
Gloria Stuart, Los Angeles: 191
Joel Finler Collection, London: 14, 16, 58b, 92b, 125, 128, 136, 143, 145 (2), 148
Slim Aarons/Getty Images, London: 152/153
Estate of John R. Hamilton, Los Angeles: 1, 5, 8/9, 11, 154, 164/165, 172 (2), 174/175, 178/179, Back Cover
Robert S. Birchard Collection, Los Angeles: 15, 22, 25, 31t, 34 (2), 41, 42, 63, 82/83, 94, 126
Everett Collection, New York: 14, 16, 30b, 36t, 37b, 38 (2), 39b, 41b, 42b, 43t, 44br, 47b, 48 (2), 68, 81, 86, 90/91, 96, 104, 112/113, 119, 137tr, 165, 166, 182 (2), 183, 184 (2), 185, 186
Photofest, New York: 10, 14, 23, 52/53, 59, 62 (2), 64t, 74b, 76/77, 78, 79 (2), 80, 83, 84t, 88, 91, 93, 98, 100r, 101, 111, 116/117, 122, 127, 139b, 150, 162t, 169, 170r, 176, 180r, 181, 190t
BiFi, Paris: 14 (2), 15 (5), 16 (3), 17 (2), 49, 103, 116, 130 (2), 162br, 163

Introduction

He is America's Homer, the man who framed the American experience for the world. He is also the most honoured of all American directors, with six Academy Awards, a man who made great films in each of five decades, from the 1920s to the 1960s.

America's humane idealism gave John Ford his themes, and his best work is energized by his recognition of his country's internal conflicts. Ford insisted that doing the right thing can and probably will get you killed, that defeat may be man's natural state, but that honour can and must be earned. His men are not leaders so much as loners, and their greatest acts are renunciations. It is no accident that, when Ford made a movie about World War Two, he made one about a campaign America lost. If one re-orders Ford's films in order of the period they portray, from the Revolutionary War of *Drums Along the Mohawk* to the televised political age of *The Last Hurrah*, it can be seen that he portrayed nearly every aspect of 200 years of America's national mythology as told by its foot-soldiers – an elegiac, driving history that Ford saw as part nostalgic fantasy and part hard-shell objective reality.

And of course there are the Westerns. Ford's Westerns have the feeling of life as well as the aura of legend. You can hear the timber creak as he combines the themes of the odyssey with his abiding sense of unkempt humanity. Ford's Westerns fulfil the essential requirement of anything lasting about America – they are about promise and, sometimes, the betrayal of promise. Ford's world is made up of soldiers and priests, of drunks and doctors and servants and whores and half-crazed men driven by their need to be alone, even as they journey toward home, toward reconciliation.

John Ford brought the art form to what still seems its ultimate synthesis of character and landscape – pictures superseding words, meanings too deep to be explained, yearnings that must remain unspoken. Most movies, even good ones, are all plot; they answer the question "What happens next?" But Ford's movies are less about what the main character will do than they are about the mysterious question of who he actually is. As even a cursory look at any of Ford's major films will reveal, he had a compositional gift that was unmatched among his peers, but he also knew how to utilize all the other intrinsic devices of the medium. He understood pacing, framing, angles, lighting. He understood characters, myth, people and, most mysteriously, he understood the cruelty of time.

OPPOSITE
On the set of 'Stagecoach' (1939)
The crew set up a shot of the Indians in front of one of The Mittens in Monument Valley.

PAGES 8/9
On the set of 'Cheyenne Autumn' (1964)
180 miles from a railway, and with only a few roads and a single telephone line, it was a great logistical feat to get horses, crew and cast set up in Monument Valley. Most lived in tents and a lucky few got to share cabins. The only shower to remove the red dust of the valley was an ice-cold water tank.

"John Ford is a poet. A comedian."
Orson Welles

ABOVE
On the set of 'Two Rode Together' (1961)
A John Ford set was always full of music. All the group shots of the company show a band of some description that would set the tone and atmosphere for a set or scene. For more than 40 years, from 'The Iron Horse' (1924) onwards, Danny Borzage (centre), brother of director Frank, would play accordion for Ford throughout the shoot. He played 'Bringing in the Sheaves' every morning when Ford arrived on the set. Accompanying Danny are James Stewart (left) on accordion and John Ford on drum.

OPPOSITE
On the set of 'Cheyenne Autumn' (1964)
One of John Ford's many idiosyncrasies on set was his habit of chewing a handkerchief. Some said it was a sign of thinking or tension, others said it was to help him cut down on his smoking. Needless to say, taking a photograph of this habit was immediate grounds for expulsion from the set. Hence, John R. Hamilton's photo was taken with a long lens to avoid detection.

His deepest moments are of memory and loss: Ma Joad burning her letters and keepsakes before leaving for California; Mayor Frank Skeffington walking home alone while the parade of the man who has beaten him moves in the opposite direction; Abe Lincoln at the grave of Ann Rutledge; Ethan Edwards exiling himself from his family and society.

Ford's Irish melancholy manifested itself in a sense of loss – for a vanished innocence, for a lost love, for a community, for a home. Many of Ford's films are large-scale, verging on the epic, but they feel intimate because they contain the same warmth, domestic detail and intimacy as his small movies. He had humour, of course, but he also had an intense and sustained gravity and feeling for the dramatic – in landscape and in people. His sense of rapport with the men and women of his movies was remarkable; Ford's is a world of genial humanity – not of cardinal sins, but of venial, hedonistic ones.

Alongside the amazing accomplishments was a singular personality: covert, with an immense charm that could turn on a dime into something dangerous. If all the stories about John Ford weren't absolutely true, it is because a lot of them were spread by him. He loved to tell stories; whether they were true or false didn't matter. "I was born in a pub in Ireland," he would say, and then this man who had been born and raised in Maine would engage in a lengthy discussion of the glories of pub life. He would claim that he reproduced the gunfight at the OK Corral exactly as it had happened, when he knew very well that he had made the whole thing up. He asserted he had worked as a cowboy in Arizona, which rather begged the question of why he was such a bad rider.

He told these stories to amuse his audience, of course, but also to amuse himself.

Mostly, Ford laid down these thickets so that he could give the impression of a physically rambunctious, horny-handed son of the soil. It was all part of the vast, comprehensive smoke-screen that was part and parcel of John Ford.

Ford delighted in pretending to be a roughneck, but his films show that he was deeply tender and sensitive. Deeply shy, he loved the physical act of making movies because it was the only thing that enabled him to come out of himself. Terrified of being found out to be a sensitive man and artist, he constructed a rocklike carapace, a character that he could play. He would be curmudgeonly, old-before-his-time Jack Ford, the man who made Westerns – half contrary, bloody-minded Irishman, half flinty New Englander, 100 percent anarchic individualist.

The point was to never let anybody know who the real John Ford was. He wanted nothing, *nothing* known of his motives, goals or inner needs. It was a front he maintained with more than due diligence, dropping it only when drunk, when he would get sloppy and sentimental.

The roots of this extraordinary talent remain elusive. His childhood had nominal creative input, based mostly around his ravenous reading, his adolescence only slightly more so. His sole aspirations were vague longings for a career in the Navy, which wasn't pursued until middle age.

Just as his artistic accomplishment carries no real competition, neither does the man. He was John Ford.

On the set of 'The Wings of Eagles' (1957)
John Ford loved stunts and stuntmen. In this stunt at the US Naval Air Station in Pensacola, Florida, John Ford is in his customary place, in front of the camera, ducking like everybody else.

13

Thematic Motifs

Abraham Lincoln

Lincoln was an iconic figure for both Francis and John Ford, who were both scholars on the subject. Older brother Francis even played the great man in several silents. John used the character in several films, and referenced him in many others. Shown are 'Young Mr. Lincoln', 'The Iron Horse', 'How the West Was Won' and 'The Prisoner of Shark Island'. Further images are on pages 110, 111 & 180.

Integration into Society

Whether by race or creed, by birth or breeding, Ford believed in fighting for the integration of his characters into the community. Shown are 'Four Sons', 'The Sun Shines Bright', 'Wagon Master' and 'The Searchers'. Further images are on pages 40, 41, 128, 129, 149 & 166.

Outsider as Thinker

The central character in a John Ford film is an outsider, somebody on the fringes of society. Sometimes he is a philosopher and thinker, often personified by the likes of Will Rogers, Henry Fonda and James Stewart. Shown are 'Doctor Bull', 'My Darling Clementine', 'Mister Roberts' and 'The Man Who Shot Liberty Valance'.

Outsider as Man of Action

The other type of outsider in a John Ford film is the man who talks with his gun and fists, typically played by Harry Carey, Victor McLaglen, John Wayne and Richard Widmark. In later films Ford explored the contrast between the thinker and man of action. Shown are 'Desperate Trails', 'The Lost Patrol', 'The Searchers' and 'Cheyenne Autumn'.

Self-Sacrifice

Throughout his career, John Ford played with the preconceptions of the audience. He believed that bad men can also have hearts and souls. In some cases, the central characters even gave their lives for others. Shown are '3 Bad Men', 'Men Without Women', 'The Prisoner of Shark Island' and '3 Godfathers'. Further images are on pages 38, 60, 91, 127, 134 & 148.

Religion

Brought up as an Irish Catholic in Maine, Ford often portrayed priests sympathetically in his films. He retained his faith throughout his life. Shown are 'The Lost Patrol', 'The Informer', 'The Fugitive' and 'Donovan's Reef'. Further images are on pages 58, 64, 65, 95 & 130.

Visual Motifs

Eating
The family, even a family of outcasts, comes together at the dinner table, often with the mother sitting at the head of the table. The absence of family members is felt. Shown are 'Four Sons', 'Stagecoach', 'The Grapes of Wrath' and 'How Green Was My Valley'.

Music and Dancing
The community comes together through music and dance. Whether formal or informal, or whether dancing with girlfriend, wife or mother, it is always a joyful event. Shown are 'The Grapes of Wrath', 'My Darling Clementine', 'Wagon Master' and 'The Sun Shines Bright'.

Drinking and Fighting
Heavy drinking and fighting are part of the bonding rituals of all-male institutions. Shown are 'How Green Was My Valley', 'Fort Apache', 'The Long Gray Line' and 'Donovan's Reef'. Further images are on pages 52/53, 56, 64, 74, 137 and 168.

Graves

As well as funerals to pay homage to the dearly departed, in several films the central character spends time at the grave talking to a loved one. Death ends a life, but not a relationship. Shown are 'Straight Shooting', 'Young Mr. Lincoln', '3 Godfathers' and 'The Searchers'. Further images are on pages 93, 111 & 137.

Doors and Fences

To be part of the family or community, the central character must be inside the door or fence. Often he leaves at the end. There is a sweet sadness at times because beyond the fence is the possibility of transcendence. Shown are 'Desperate Trails', 'Drums Along the Mohawk', 'She Wore a Yellow Ribbon' and 'The Searchers'.

The Irish

John Ford once said to playwright Eugene O'Neill, "If there is any single thing that explains either of us, it's that we're Irish." Although Ford was born in America into an Irish family, his sensibilities and poetic soul were definitely Irish. Shown are 'Mother Machree', 'The Informer', 'The Quiet Man' and 'The Rising of the Moon'. Other films with Irish settings include 'Hangman's House', 'The Plough and the Stars' and 'Young Cassidy'. Further images are on pages 65, 67, 94, 95, 100, 144–147, 163.

On the Trail
1894–1927

John A. Feeney, the father of the man whom the world would come to know as John Ford, was born in the village of Spiddal, in County Galway, Ireland, on 15 June 1854. In 1875, three years after he came to America, where the opportunities were far greater and the English heel was off their collective necks, Feeney married Barbara Curran, known to family and friends as Abby. The year after he was married, John Feeney became a father, and he continued to become a father. There were 11 children in all, five of them dying in infancy.

John Ford always claimed to have been born Sean Aloysius O'Fearna – or some equally florid variant – on 1 February 1895. And for ninety-odd years he was taken at his word. But the registry of births for Cape Elizabeth, Maine clearly records the birth of one John Martin Feeney on 1 February 1894 – the date on his birth registration, on his school records at Portland High School and on his death certificate.

The subtraction of a year from Jack's age stemmed from a childhood bout of diphtheria that caused him to lose a year at school, while his reasons for Gaelicizing his name were almost certainly because it made him feel more Irish, more authentic.

The elder John Feeney opened a grocery store, at 42 Center Street in Portland, Maine, that was really a front for an illegal saloon (Maine was a dry state). The Feeney 'grocery store' was a success, and he opened up four more in the following years. The saloons became gathering places where John would meet new immigrants from Ireland, help them settle, find jobs and register them as God-fearing voters for the Democratic Party.

John Martin Feeney, commonly known as Jack, was a bruising fullback and defensive tackle on the Portland High state championship football team. Young Feeney was known by the ominous nickname "Bull" because of his habit of lowering his helmet and charging through the line like a maddened bull.

Academically, young Jack was what would now be termed an underachiever. His report card from the Emerson School for 1905-06 listed Reading (next to film-making, the great passion of his life) vacillating from Fair to Good, Arithmetic ping-ponging from Poor to Good, Geography going from Poor to Excellent. He could do anything he set his mind to but he chose not to set his mind to academic excellence.

With some justification, Ford would claim extenuating circumstances. "I was a good student," he would tell his grandson Dan Ford and Katharine Hepburn. "I

On the set of an unknown film (1919)
Harry Carey and Jack Ford had an intense four-year working relationship. They would go out into the hills of Newhall, north of Hollywood, and live rough with the crew, making up stories and filming stunts as they went along. Only three of their 25 films from this period have survived complete: 'Straight Shooting', 'Bucking Broadway' and 'Hell Bent'.

"The difference between John Ford and other directors is the difference between Gulliver and the little people who tied him down."

George Peppard

Family picture
A young John Martin Feeney (later John Ford) dressed as a sailor. Ford's love of the sea would come to fruition through his films (several have naval subjects), through his 106-foot ketch, the 'Araner', and through his work for the United States Navy during World War Two, where he rose to the rank of rear admiral in the United States Naval Reserve.

never took a book home because I had to work in the morning, sprint all the way to school, go to school and then go out on the athletic field, then at night I worked in the theatre."

Jack was indeed stage-struck; he would tell Kate Hepburn that after the second performance of any play in Portland, he could begin to repeat the lines. Even more than the theatre, however, there were the movies. Whenever he got a nickel, he went to the nickelodeon. What he loved the most were Westerns.

He was already an avid reader; a classmate named Oscar Vanier would remember that "Every time you'd see him, he'd have a book in his hand, Shakespeare or something. He'd fight at the drop of a hat, but he had a great mind and a great sense of humour. Someone would tell him a funny story, and the next day [he] would retell it, adding all kinds of new touches to it."

He was also responsible; at the age of 15, Jack took out a $500 insurance policy payable to his mother in the event of his death. (Years later Ford would cast Sara Allgood as the unprepossessing but dominant mother in *How Green Was My Valley* (1941) because she reminded him of Abby Feeney. "She looked like my mother and I made her act like my mother.")

Among the Feeney sons, the black sheep was Francis or, as he was generally known, Frank. He was born on 14 August 1881, dropped out of high school at 17 and served in the Maine infantry during the Spanish-American War. Afterwards, he returned to Portland and got a local girl pregnant. There was a shotgun wedding, followed closely by the marriage breaking up. Frank left Portland and became an actor.

Frank achieved stardom in a series of films for the pioneer producer Thomas Ince under the name Francis Ford. He changed his name because it was a better stage name and less ethnic. In *Blazing the Trail* (1912) and *The Struggle* (1913), for example, Frank made movies that were quite authentic, often sympathetic to Indians, often concerned with the details of military life on the frontier.

In Hollywood, Frank earned a reputation as a talented but flighty and tempestuous character, with a mighty thirst. At Universal, from 1913 to 1916, he produced and directed about eighty films, plus four serials. From April 1914, Ford and Grace Cunard became, along with Pearl White, the leading serial stars of the era.

Back home in Portland, Jack graduated from high school in June of 1914. His overall grade average was 84.9, just missing a B; he earned three letters in football and twice won Honourable Mention on the Maine all-state team. After graduation, Jack made his way west to bum a summer vacation off his older brother. By August, he was playing a small part in *The Mysterious Rose* (1914), one of Frank's movies. College was put on the back burner. In the November 1914 issue of *The Racquet*, Portland High's alumni bulletin, there is this brief notation: 'John Feeney is closely connected with the Universal Film Company at Hollywood, California.'

Soon afterwards, for the sake of convenience and to take advantage of whatever nepotistic connections could be made, Jack adopted the same last name as his brother. Jack "Bull" Feeney was now Jack Ford.

Although Ford would spend the rest of his life in the movies, he never left Portland behind, either literally – he visited nearly every year – or emotionally. Jack Ford would always emphasize his Irishness – indeed, he was a professional Irishman – so most commentators and critics followed his lead. But he was also that staunchest of New Englanders, a Maine man, with an abiding memory of the New England town, that is to say an ideal community of enduring values.

ABOVE
Family picture
Cousin John Connelly with the Feeney brothers:
Edward (Eddie), Francis (Frank) and John
(Jack). Each of the Feeney brothers went into the
film business. First Frank became successful
actor/director Francis Ford. John learned the
business as an assistant to Francis before
becoming a director and adopting the name Jack
Ford. Eddie, who took the surname O'Fearna to
distinguish himself from his brothers, worked as
an assistant director on many of Jack's films.

LEFT
Portland High School
John "Bull" Feeney (top row, far right) was the
star fullback of the 1913 state champion football
team. His love of sport extended into later life:
Ford befriended and employed football players
like Wardell "Ward" Bond, Marion "Duke"
Morrison (later John Wayne) and Woody Strode;
and football and baseball found their way into
films like 'Salute', 'Up the River', 'Rookie of the
Year' and 'Flashing Spikes'.

From Portland, Jack learned the value of the common people, the beauty of the natural world, and the transcendent symmetry that results when the two are joined together. He felt the lure of the sea and the unspoken bonds that hold working men together. He saw the wrecks off Portland Head Light, the catastrophe that can result when good men are overwhelmed by fate, and the dignity of the women who waited while their men went down to the sea in ships.

Beyond that, his Maine upbringing had given him a valuable lesson in modesty, for you do not put on airs if you live in Maine; the worst thing a Yankee can be is a snob. He had, in short, learned the emotional dynamic that would inform practically every film he would ever make.

Surviving stills show John Ford working as an actor in some of his brother's films. Mostly, though, he was a general dogsbody around Universal, doing what he was told, working as a carpenter, prop man, editor, assistant cameraman, assistant director or stunt man. He was whatever Frank wanted him to be. He was learning the movie business from the ground up, learning all the facets of it as a craft, without which no art is possible.

He continued to see every movie he could, especially if it was directed by D.W. Griffith, and would later assert that "The showing of those early pictures in the old Philharmonic Auditorium in Los Angeles meant more to the film industry and to the making of Hollywood than all the spectacles of inauguration that Hollywood promotes in these later days and nights."

He learned the mechanics and optics of a camera; he learned to prize the invaluable craftspeople, the unassuming blue-collar backbone of movie-making. He learned how a good director inspires loyalty and devotion.

So it was that John Ford was ready when opportunity presented itself, as it surely was bound to, for in the years around World War One, Hollywood was in expansionist mode, continually ramping up production to meet a demand that just kept growing. Trade paper reviews prove that he even starred in a couple of now-lost two-reelers. Nudging opportunity along was the fact that the bulk of Universal's product was bread-and-butter movies – Westerns in the 1910s and 1920s, horror films in the 1930s.

Among the actors populating Carl Laemmle's Westerns was Henry DeWitt Carey II, born in Harlem, New York in 1878. The son of a White Plains judge, Carey had been enraptured by the lurid dime novels that began the legend of the West. After an abortive fling with law school, Carey drifted into writing and acting. He made his first film in 1908 for D. W. Griffith – he can be seen in a prominent part in *The Musketeers of Pig Alley* (1912), Griffith's famous proto-gangster film.

There are several variant versions of how Ford made the jump to director. Ford's version, repeated to Peter Bogdanovich and others, was that he was pressed into service as a prop director, working without film in the camera, to impress Carl Laemmle, who had suddenly appeared from New York. "A little later," Ford said, "they needed a director for a two-reeler, and Laemmle said, 'Try Ford. He yells loud.'"

It's a viable scenario, but there's an alternate version, in which brother Frank was the pivotal figure. "Francis came to [Harry Carey] one day," remembered Olive Carey, Harry's wife and a close Ford friend, "and said, 'My kid brother is here… I think he'd be a hell of a director.' So Harry said, 'Well, bring him around.' So that's how they met and they just clicked."

ABOVE
Still from 'The Birth of a Nation' (1915)
Jack Ford was an extra in D. W. Griffith's silent epic. He said that he rode a horse, constantly holding up his hood so that he could see with his glasses, much like the rider on the right. Griffith was one of Ford's major influences as a director.

OPPOSITE
Still from 'Peg o' the Ring' (1916)
As well as completing his duties as prop man, stunt man and assistant director on his brother Frank's films, Jack (left) also acted in several of them.

ABOVE
Still from 'Smuggler's Island' (1915)
Generally Jack Ford (left) acted as a henchman in his brother's films. Here Grace Cunard is being menaced by Harry Schumm after she accidentally discovers the smuggler's secret lair.

RIGHT
Still from 'Peg o' the Ring' (1916)
The speed of filming meant that Jack Ford (left) sometimes forgot to check his costume. On one film it is reported that could be seen on the screen dancing with a hammer protruding from his back pocket. However, he was well thought of as a property man – when needed, Ford would empty nearby houses of furniture to dress the set.

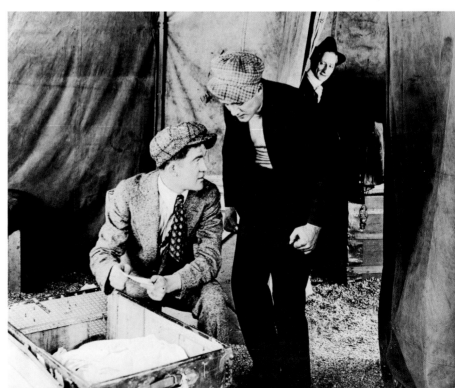

On the set of 'The Broken Coin' (1915)
Director Francis Ford (left) with actors Grace
Cunard (as Kitty Gray) and Eddie Polo (Roleau)
in front of the camera. In this 22-part serial,
released weekly starting on 21 June 1915, Kitty
Gray discovers half a coin and sets off in search
of a vast treasure. As evidence of the informal
nature of these early silent films, everybody
contributed to the film both on and off screen.
Grace Cunard also wrote the serial. Francis Ford
played Count Frederick. Jack Ford (in
characteristic pose to the right of the camera,
wearing his trademark cap) was an assistant and
played Count Sacchio's accomplice.

Stills from 'Straight Shooting' (1917)
From his very first feature film, John Ford's use of the camera to frame actors (middle) and to give effective close-ups (bottom, Harry Carey) was already extant. He also had a vivid sense of place, as can be seen by the famous pass in Newhall (top), called Beale's Cut, which also appeared in 'Three Jumps Ahead' (see page 47), 'The Iron Horse' and 'Stagecoach'. His brother Francis was a great influence on his film style.

Whoever provided the impetus, Carey gazed upon a young man, six feet tall, with lots of deep red hair, and glasses to even out his near-sightedness. Ford and Carey would make more than 20 pictures over the next four years, and for a time Ford even lived with Carey and his wife at their little house in Newhall.

"They weren't shoot-em-ups," Ford would recall of these early movies, in which Carey played a modest, shambling saddle tramp rather than a bold gunfighter. "They were character stories. Carey was a great actor… he always wore a dirty blue shirt and an old vest, patched overalls, very seldom carried a gun – and he didn't own a hat. On each picture, the cowboys would line up and he'd go down the line and finally pick one of their hats and wear that; it would please the owner because it meant he worked through all that picture… All this was fifty percent Carey and fifty percent me."

Ford and Carey fell into an easy working rhythm, and Ford watched the older man work and noted the economy with which he got his effects. "I learned a great deal from Harry," remembered Ford. "He was a slow-moving actor when he was afoot. You could read his mind, peer into his eyes and see him think."

Jack and Harry would shoot their films off-the-cuff, then a friend named George Hively would bang out an after-the-fact script so that the front office would be happy. In off moments, Jack would draw sketches – good ones – of Western or Indian faces on the back of script pages.

Most of Ford's early films haven't survived, but those that have are instructive. *Straight Shooting* (1917), Ford's earliest surviving feature, shows that he had already developed components of his great talent, specifically his gift for landscape. The compositions, usually in deep focus, have balance, depth and spaciousness, and Ford easily constructs natural frames out of a tree and some foreground bushes. Interior sets were built on location, so authentic backgrounds can be glimpsed through windows and doorways. The performances are easy and natural, with less gesticulation than was normal for the period; there are naturalistic tics scattered through the film, as in Harry Carey's lack of a gun belt. (His gun is tucked into his pants.)

Straight Shooting reflects some of the sober austerity of the William S. Hart Westerns that were all the rage, but that was unavoidable because Hart was the only star making major Westerns. But if the *Shane*-like plot is a clear echo of Hart, the level of production polish is considerably greater than comparable films from Universal, and certainly greater than you'd expect from a director making his first feature after quickly matriculating in slam-bang two-reelers, where there was no time for characterization, only story.

And there are fascinating foreshadowings of much later films. In the end, Cheyenne Harry touches on aspects of Tom Doniphon in *The Man Who Shot Liberty Valance*, as he experiences a deep sense of melancholy by helping homesteaders who will inevitably destroy his way of life. Harry's loneliness, his idea of himself as an outsider who can only cross the threshold of a home as a guest, will also be seen in Ethan Edwards, in Ford's great, savage *The Searchers*.

The film already reflects the sober, uncondescending approach that Ford would bring to Westerns. It looks more like a movie from 1922 or 1923 than one from 1917, and in an art form that moved as torrentially as the movies did in their infancy, that is no small statement.

Bucking Broadway (1917), made shortly after *Straight Shooting*, again stars Harry Carey. Cheyenne Harry is marrying the boss' daughter, and, just like John Wayne's

ABOVE
Still from 'Straight Shooting' (1917)
Carey and Ford tried to be more realistic than the
other screen cowboys. Most cowboys could not
shoot straight with a pistol so they preferred a
rifle, which was more accurate. Also Carey often
played a saddle tramp rather than the heroic
gunfighter of the pulps.

PAGES 28/29
On the set of 'A Marked Man' (1917)
Jack Ford (right) films a hold-up. During this
period he learned to hold a film in his head and
to only shoot the angles that he wanted to use,
often on the first take. He later said an editor
should only have to cut the ends off the film and
splice the bits together in the right order. This
method was a very quick and cheap way of
making films. It also meant that the film could
only be cut together one way, as Ford saw it. In
this scene, bandit Cheyenne Harry (Harry Carey,
not present) protests when the driver is shot.
Later, Cheyenne is sentenced to hang for the
murder. A lost film.

ABOVE
Still from 'The Scarlet Drop' (1918)
Kaintuck Cass (Harry Carey, centre) is
considered trash by aristocrat Molly Calvert
(Molly Malone, left), but they fall in love. Love
across the class divide is a theme that reoccurs
throughout Ford's films. A lost film.

RIGHT
Still from 'A Marked Man' (1917)
Cheyenne Harry (Harry Carey) is sentenced to
hang, but is given two weeks grace so that he
can pretend to his visiting mother that he has a
wife and ranch. Molly Young (Molly Malone)
agrees to be his wife. A lost film.

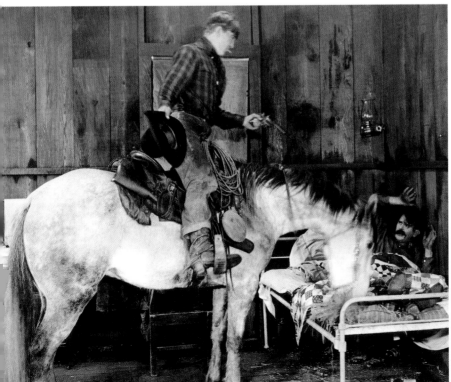

ABOVE
Still from 'Three Mounted Men' (1918)
Cheyenne Harry (Harry Carey) is released from prison to find Buck Masters. He arranges for Buck to be arrested, but when Harry finds out that Lola (Neva Gerber) is Buck's sister, he rescues Buck from the police. A lost film.

LEFT
Still from 'Hell Bent' (1918)
Cheyenne Harry (Harry Carey, left) persuades Cimarron Bill (Duke Lee) to share a room with him (and his horse?) when everywhere else is full.

"It was the vision that set him apart. The photographic eye. And the total knowledge and love of the people he was working with. He could look at a thing and compose it as well as Cézanne. All great directors can do that, but [George] Stevens and [Alfred] Hitchcock would have had their Cézannes all around them in sketch form. Ford's Cézannes wouldn't be seen until he did it, because it was in his head. Those others were architects. Ford was a wonderfully fluid painter."

Rod Taylor

Still from 'Hell Bent' (1918)
This atmospheric still gives an idea of the painterly attention to detail that John Ford and his cinematographers (Ben Reynolds and John W. Brown) got into their Western scenes. They often took their cues from the paintings of Frederic Remington and Charles M. Russell.

ABOVE
Still from 'The Fighting Brothers' (1919)
Sheriff Pete Larkin (Pete Morrison, right) hunts
down and captures his brother Lonnie (Hoot
Gibson), who is wanted for murder. However,
once he establishes that Lonnie is innocent, they
both go on the run. A lost film.

RIGHT
On the set of 'The Horse Soldiers' (1959)
Ed "Hoot" Gibson and John Ford, who used to
be roommates, share a moment together. Hoot, a
rodeo cowboy-turned-actor, started his acting
career in 1910, and went on to become a stunt
man for Harry Carey before joining John Ford's
Stock Company.

ABOVE
Still from 'A Fight for Love' (1919)
Cheyenne Harry (Harry Carey, centre) chats to
Kate McDougall (Neva Gerber) in front of his rival
in love Black Michael (Joe Harris). A lost film.

LEFT
On the set of 'A Fight for Love' (1919)
California's Big Bear region substituted for
Canada, where Cheyenne Harry and Black
Michael are pursued by the Mounties. In this
photo John Ford and photographer John W.
Brown are to the left of the camera, whilst Harry
Carey and J. Farrell MacDonald (as a priest) are
in front of them. MacDonald was part of Ford's
Stock Company, notching up more appearances
than anybody else except Jack Pennick, Harry
Tenbrook and Francis Ford. Note the musicians,
who provided a suitable atmosphere for the
actors.

RIGHT
Still from 'Riders of Vengeance' (1919)
Cheyenne Harry (Harry Carey) kills the people who murdered his bride and her parents on his wedding day, until only Sheriff Gale Thurman is left. Harry considers killing Thurman's girl (Seena Owen) but falls in love with her after caring for her in his cave hideout. A lost film.

BELOW
Still from 'Riders of Vengeance' (1919)
Harry keeps a steady aim on Buell (J. Farrell MacDonald, left), who is talking to Sheriff Gale Thurman (Joe Harris).

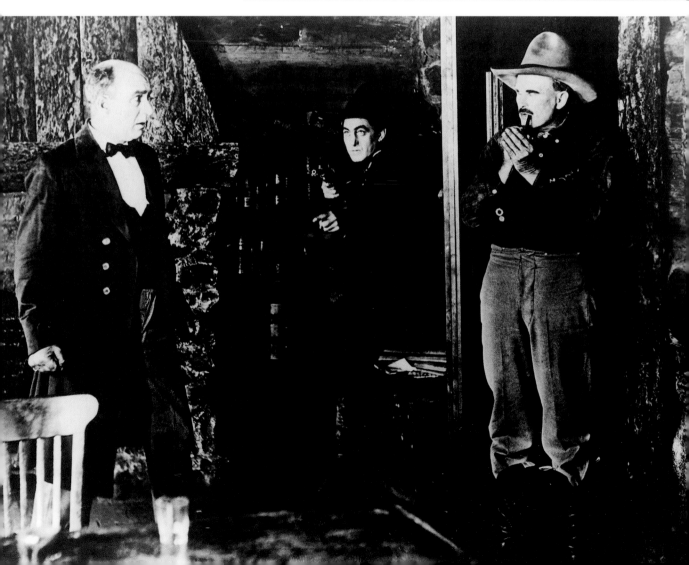

Tom Doniphon in *The Man Who Shot Liberty Valance*, he has quietly saved up enough money to build a home for his new bride. But she is spirited off to New York by a city slicker, and Harry and his cowpoke friends kill two birds with one stone by taking some cattle to the railroad yards in the big city and getting the girl back in the process.

The film has more plot than its running time can accommodate – Ford simply skips the actual cattle drive. Although the locations are clearly shot on the Universal backlot, Ford's confidence is building; he frames far more elaborate compositions than he had only months before. In particular, he uses three-tiered landscapes: a rider in the foreground, a stream of cattle passing in the middle distance, and some riders on a ridge at the horizon line. Visually, the film is far more sophisticated than its narrative, but it wouldn't be long before Fordian theme and Fordian image coalesced.

By Indian Post (aka *The Love Letter*, 1919), another surviving early Ford film, was a two-reeler, although only one reel survives. The interiors are ordinary, but the locations immediately leap to life – cowboys splash across a picturesque river, and you can practically feel the spray.

The trade papers began using phrases about Ford's films that had heretofore been reserved for Frank's: "Thrilling…teeming with life and color and action." The *Universal Weekly* wrote that, "For a long time people have said, as they heard the name 'Ford' in connection with a picture: 'Ford? Any relation to Francis?' Very soon, unless all indications of the present time fail, they will be saying, 'Ford? Any relation to Jack?'"

In these years, Ford was mostly flying beneath the publicity radar – undoubtedly the way he wanted it. Likewise, the New York critics couldn't be bothered with anything as *déclassé* as Westerns; *The New York Times* didn't review a single John Ford movie before 1922, and even after that ignored some of his pictures.

The pictures Ford was making were unpretentious programmers, and the Universal films that critics were interested in were by the studio's eccentric, brilliant young directors like Erich von Stroheim and Tod Browning. Jack Ford was cranking them out: seven features in 1918, nine in 1919, plus a few two-reelers thrown in for good measure. Production schedules averaged no more than a week or so for a two-reeler, two to three weeks for a five-reel feature.

But Ford's bread-and-butter pictures were only paying him bread-and-butter money – about $300 a week. It was time to move on, and in December 1920, Jack Ford left Universal and went to work for William Fox. It was not the only change in his life that year. In March, he had met a young nurse named Mary McBryde Smith at a St Patrick's Day dance thrown by the director Rex Ingram. "We met that night with Rex," Mary would remember years later, "and we saw each other every day after that, and just naturally got married. Just naturally."

They wed on 3 July 1920, and in October they moved to a house at 6860 Odin Street in Hollywood – stone-built, with leaded windows, situated on a hill behind the Hollywood Bowl, where the music from the concerts would waft over the four acres of wild gardens. The Fords lived in the Odin Street house for 34 years. Nine months to the day after the wedding, Patrick Michael Roper Ford was born, and on 16 December 1922, there was another child, Barbara Nugent Ford.

Ford's reasons for signing with Fox were both financial and creative; his salary doubled, from $13,618 to $27,891. Besides that, Fox was on the brink of a building

ABOVE
Still from 'Rider of the Law' (1919)
Texas Ranger Jim Kyneton (Harry Carey) puts duty before his love for Betty (Gloria Hope). A lost film.

TOP
Still from 'The Outcasts of Poker Flat' (1919)
In the story within a story, John Oakhurst (Harry Carey) befriends a suicidal woman on a steamboat and takes her home to marry his son. A lost film.

ABOVE
Still from 'Marked Men' (1919)
Train robbers Cheyenne Harry, Bill and Tom escape from prison and then rob a bank. A lost film.

RIGHT
Still from 'Marked Men' (1919)
Whilst on the run in the desert, the criminals adopt a baby when its mother dies. This Peter B. Kyne short story has been filmed several times. Even Ford remade it in 1948 as '3 Godfathers'.

"[Harry] Carey was a great actor."

John Ford

ABOVE
Still from 'Hitchin' Posts' (1920)
Jefferson Todd (Frank Mayo) is a Southern
gentleman who falls on bad times but retains his
honour, even when he has to duel his evil
brother-in-law. A lost film.

TOP LEFT
On the set of 'The Girl in Number 29' (1920)
Jack Ford gives direction to Ray Ripley, who
plays Abdullah the strangler. A lost film.

LEFT
Still from 'The Last Outlaw' (1919)
Idaleen Coburn (Lucille Hutton) is caught in the
clutches of a bootlegger, but she is rescued by
her father, an old outlaw just released from jail. A
lost film.

Still from 'Just Pals' (1920)
Bim (Buck Jones, centre) is the town bum, who takes responsibility for child hobo Bill (George E. Stone, left). After they prevent a robbery and save the reputation of schoolteacher Mary Bruce (Helen Ferguson, right), Bim is no longer considered an outsider. The outsider validated through brave actions and plain speaking is a persona that runs through many of Ford's films, whether played by Will Rogers or Henry Fonda or James Stewart.

programme that William Fox intended would put his studio on an equivalent footing with Paramount – the industry leader in the early 1920s.

Ford's first film for Fox was a good one, and it has survived. *Just Pals* (1920) is essentially a Harry Carey vehicle that stars the up-and-coming Fox star Buck Jones, and it contains all the qualities that were already characteristic of Ford: folksy, well-observed characters in a setting rife with Americana, in this case a town on the border between Wyoming and Nebraska.

Jones plays the town's good-for-nothing layabout. "Wanna earn two bits?" he is asked. "I got two bits," he says. Bim is a gentle soul who can't bring himself to kill a chicken, and he loves the schoolteacher from afar. By dint of some melodramatic plot machinations, Bim saves the schoolteacher from an embezzling charge, reunites a young hobo with his parents and earns a rich reward. When last seen, he is walking in the woods with the schoolteacher and the townspeople have learned the error of their original low estimation of him. Bim's life as an outcast is over.

Narratively, *Just Pals* is of nominal interest, but visually it's fascinating. Already Ford is making the landscape a character. *Just Pals* is full of dappled light and shade, leaves moving softly in the breeze, gently rolling landscapes revealed in quiet pans and tracking shots. It probably gives a good idea of what Ford's films at Universal were like – confident and relaxed, with an understated lyrical touch, a sense of

ABOVE
Still from 'The Freeze Out' (1921)
Ohio, the Stranger (Harry Carey, right) arrives in
Broken Buckle and starts building a gambling
house to rival Headling Whipple's. However,
when he falls in love with Whipple's sister Zoe,
who disapproves of gambling, Ohio turns the
building into a school and library. Ford shows the
civilising of the Wild West, as he later would in
'My Darling Clementine'. A lost film.

LEFT
Still from 'The Big Punch' (1921)
Buck (Buck Jones, left) wants to go to a
theological seminary but his brother Jed gets
mixed up with bad Flash McGraw (George
Siegmann, right). After a spell in jail for a crime
he did not commit, Buck becomes a priest. A
lost film.

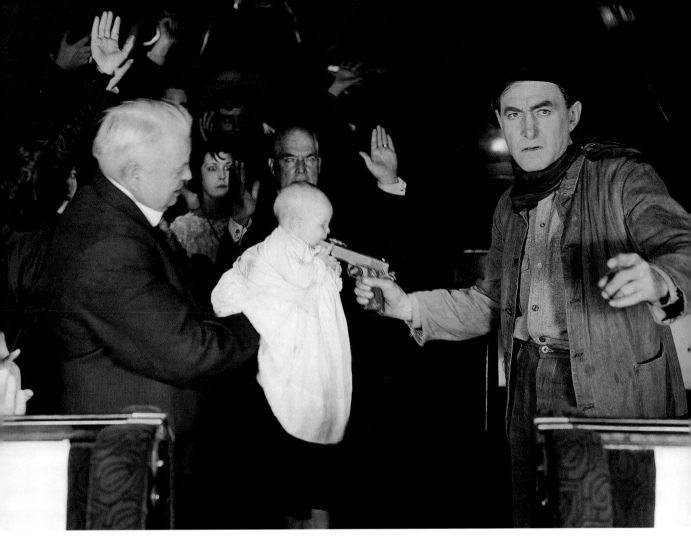

ABOVE
Still from 'Desperate Trails' (1921)
Bert Carson (Harry Carey, right) loves Lady Lou and goes to jail to protect her brother. After finding out the 'brother' is Lady Lou's lover, Bert escapes from jail and kills him. A lost film.

RIGHT
Still from 'The Wallop' (1921)
John Wesley Pringle (Harry Carey) makes a strike at his mine and when he goes back home, he finds that the girl he loves is in love with another man. After helping the girl's boyfriend defeat the local sheriff, John goes back to his mine. A lost film.

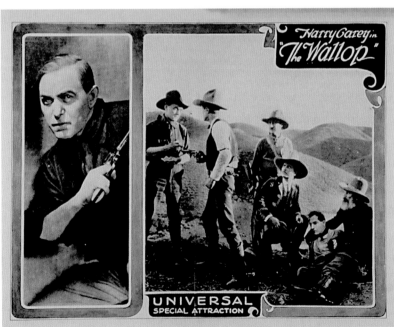

"If I had my way, every morning of my life I'd be behind that camera at nine o'clock waiting for the boys to roll 'em, because that's the only thing I really like to do."

John Ford

Publicity still for 'Sure Fire' (1921)
Marian Hoffman (Molly Malone) thinks her boyfriend Jeff Bransford (Hoot Gibson) doesn't have ambition, but his bravery nets them $5,000 by the end of the story. A lost film.

Still from 'Action' (1921)
Sandy Brooke (Hoot Gibson, second left), Mormon Peters (J. Farrell MacDonald, second right) and Soda Water Manning (Francis Ford, right) take an interest in orphan Molly (Clara Horton) because she is the heir to a ranch and mine. The three godfathers end up in jail while Molly is at school, but when she returns she sorts everything out. A lost film.

HOOT GIBSON in "ACTION"
Universal Special Feature Production~

domestic detail and a protective sense of humanity that only a few directors of the period (D.W. Griffith, Maurice Tourneur) could touch. As Lindsay Anderson would write of *Just Pals*, 'For all the artifice of its plotting, the way people behave is real; feelings are experienced, not just represented, and in this way the stereotypes are brought to life.' It was a comment that could serve as critical shorthand for all of Ford's best work for the next quarter-century.

Just Pals also puts in place one of Ford's primary themes: the superiority of people on society's margins to mainstream solid citizens. Take away the melodrama and it is a Will Rogers picture, nearly the equal of *Judge Priest*, fourteen years later.

The critics noticed, and so did William Fox. '*Just Pals*,' Fox wrote, 'was one of the most artistically done pictures that I have reviewed in years… Ford has proven that if Jones is properly directed he can play any part.'

Ford was put into harness directing Fox's mainstays, rural melodramas and Westerns, including several with Tom Mix, the primary Western star of the 1920s. He continued his ascent with *Cameo Kirby* (1923), an adaptation of a play by Booth Tarkington and Harry Leon Wilson. But Ford was always indifferent to the conventions of stage melodrama, and he directed *Cameo Kirby* on autopilot. There is some atmospheric photography, there is the dashing John Gilbert, shortly before he became a matinee idol at MGM, and there is the first, indistinct appearance of a

ABOVE
Still from 'The Village Blacksmith' (1922)
Based on Henry Wadsworth Longfellow's poem, here John Hammond (William Walling) confronts Squire Ezra Brigham (Tully Marshall). A lost film.

OPPOSITE TOP
Still from 'Jackie' (1921)
Dancer Jackie (Shirley Mason) escapes to London with crippled Benny and is saved by rich Mervyn Carter (William Scott). A lost film.

OPPOSITE BOTTOM LEFT
Still from 'Silver Wings' (1922)
Jack Ford directed the prologue, which contains an emotional scene when the baby dies. A lost film.

OPPOSITE BOTTOM RIGHT
Still from 'Little Miss Smiles' (1922)
In this tale of a Jewish family living in a New York ghetto, Ford mixes broad humour and nervy drama, as seen through the eyes of Esther Aaronson (Shirley Mason, on bed). A lost film.

ABOVE
Still from 'The Face on the Barroom Floor' (1923)
Whilst in Maine with his fiancé, respected artist Robert Stevens (Henry B. Walthall) paints fisherman's daughter Lottie (Alma Bennett). Lottie commits suicide and Stevens is blamed, although he is innocent. His life is ruined and he becomes a derelict. A lost film.

RIGHT
Still from 'The Face on the Barroom Floor' (1923)
Many years later, Stevens is reunited with his socialite fiancé Marion Von Vleck (Ruth Clifford).

ABOVE
Still from 'Three Jumps Ahead' (1923)
Steve Clancy (Tom Mix) and his uncle Virgil (Francis Ford) are captured by outlaws and forced to work in their mine. When one of the prisoners escapes, Steve is forced to recapture him or his uncle will die. A lost film.

LEFT
Still from 'Cameo Kirby' (1923)
Cameo Kirby (John Gilbert, right) is a riverboat gambler who wins the estate of Colonel Randall (William E. Lawrence) to save him from Colonel Moreau. This is the first film to be directed by 'John' rather than 'Jack' Ford.

ABOVE
Still from 'North of Hudson Bay' (1923)
The climax of the film featured a canoe chase but since Tom Mix and John Ford were the only two people who could paddle a canoe, Ford dressed up in furs and carried out the stunts with Mix.

RIGHT
Still from 'North of Hudson Bay' (1923)
Michael Dane (Tom Mix) falls in love with Estelle MacDonald (Kathleen Kay) on the way out to his brother's gold mine.

Still from 'Hoodman Blind' (1923)
After rescuing his wife from a sinking boat, Jack Yeulette (David Butler, right) confronts crooked lawyer Mark Lezzard (Frank Campeau). A lost film.

young actress named Jean Arthur, but there is also a great deal of rote interiors. At this stage of his career, Ford's feel for landscape was leagues ahead of his interest in interiors.

It was with *Cameo Kirby* that Ford felt dignity creeping up on him. Although his friends would call him Jack to his dying day, for public consumption his billing was no longer Jack Ford. From *Cameo Kirby* on, he was professionally known as John Ford.

In 1923, Paramount had an unexpected blockbuster with James Cruze's *The Covered Wagon*, the film that fired the starting gun for the Western epic. William Fox was determined to top it. *The Covered Wagon* told of the courage and hardships of the pioneers of the late 1840s; Fox determined to make a film about the post-Civil War building of the transcontinental railroad, which rendered such wagon trains obsolete.

The project was called *The Iron Horse* (1924), and Ford campaigned hard for the assignment. Although only 31 years old, he had amassed a considerable body of work: a dozen two-reelers and over 35 features, far more finished film than any

"When a motion picture is at its best, it is long on action and short on dialogue. When it tells its story and reveals its characters in a series of simple, beautiful, active pictures, and does it with as little talk as possible, then the motion picture medium is being used to its fullest advantage."

John Ford

On the set of 'The Iron Horse' (1924)
For this epic production, an unheated, flea-ridden circus train was hired to house the cast and crew but it was so cold in the Sierra Nevada (there were constant blizzards) that they all started living in the makeshift sets. Ford maintained discipline and morale, leading his troops like a general. Every morning a bugler (prop man and World War One veteran Herbert "Limey" Plews, centre) announced reveille. There were football games on the weekend and entertainment at night.

modern director can hope to accomplish in his working life. He had demonstrated an expertise with the West and its characters. William Fox could have spent extra money to bring in a prestige director from outside, but he could hardly have done better than young John Ford.

Ford began production of *The Iron Horse* in Mexico, doubled back to New Mexico then went to Dodge, Nevada, where most of the film was actually made. The company rented Pullman cars from a circus to house the cast and crew.

The film was made under difficult conditions. It was winter and bitter cold. Not only that, but Ford was shooting blind, shipping each day's work to Hollywood where it could be developed. By the time he saw a day's work, it could be a week later, making retakes difficult. Besides that, the boxcar that held the projection room was so cold nobody wanted to go in it. The result was that Ford never saw a foot of the film he was shooting and had to keep the entire picture in his mind.

The weather was a constant factor. A scene would begin in normal conditions, but during the night it would snow and at dawn the entire company would be out with shovels and brooms, moving the snow out of camera range so they could begin shooting by 9:00 or 9:30. The unit had their own bootlegger and, after a time, their own brothel. Ford and company weren't making a Western: they were living it.

This communal, off-the-cuff quality of location life would come to be prized by Ford. It was catch-as-catch-can, away from the hated front office. It forced Ford to rely on his instincts, and forced the large crew to look to Ford for guidance.

The circumstances of the production couldn't help but bring a sense of reality to the picture, which was one of the things that the critics hailed when the film premiered in August 1924. *The Iron Horse* introduced the element of the epic into Ford's work – vast open spaces, and characters who are heroes because of what they do in the face of attack and hostile natural elements, all combined with a dramatic story and intimate characterizations.

The young John Ford allowed only trace elements of sombre melancholy to intrude on *The Iron Horse* – it was, after all, about the successful unification of a nation. Ford kept his eye on the big picture, intent on his ultimate goal: to direct a moving historical romance about the country he loved, peopled by those with whom he felt a kinship: the labourer, the mechanic, the engineer, all in the service of a vision of American progress.

It is the locations that make *The Iron Horse*, giving the film its documentary air – you can't capture Manifest Destiny in a studio. When horses storm into town, their breath and the condensation from their bodies nearly obliterate the figures of the

Still from 'The Iron Horse' (1924)
The film not only showed the joining of America through the transcontinental railroad, but also the sweat and tears of the ethnic groups who made it happen. Irish, Italian and Chinese intermingle. The conflict between the Irish and Italian communities is treated humorously. Ford's rough humour, which became one of his trademark touches, sometimes grates on the sensibilities of modern critics, but it seems authentic. Several of the Chinese workers in the film had made the real railroad and served as technical consultants.

Still from 'The Iron Horse' (1924)
Davy Brandon (George O'Brien) and Deroux (Fred Kohler) in the climactic fight, which takes place as Indians, incited by Deroux, attack the railroad. Deroux had killed Davy's father many years earlier, and is trying to divert the railroad through land that he owns. Ford would later perfect this idea of foregrounding personal stories on a canvas of epic landscapes in films like 'Stagecoach' and 'Wagon Master'. This was George O'Brien's first leading role, the first of six for Ford, although he remained in Ford's Stock Company with cameos until 1964.

ABOVE
On the set of 'The Iron Horse' (1924)
Holes were dug for cameras to film stampeding
buffalo and galloping horses. Two buffaloes fell
into the hole, but the crew continued filming.
Before cinematographer George Schneiderman,
operator Burnett Guffey and director Ford filmed
the horses, Ford instructed his brother Eddie:
"After the scene, if you don't hear any noise from
in here, don't bother to look – just fill it up with
dirt."

LEFT
Still from 'The Iron Horse' (1924)
After defeating the Indian attack, the railroaders
make a sad return to their makeshift town,
nursing their wounded and mourning their dead.
On the eve of the railroad's completion, the true
cost of the endeavour is brought home to the
workers.

ABOVE
Still from 'Lightnin'' (1925)
Mother Jones (Madge Bellamy) withholds the
demon drink from Lightnin' Bill Jones (Jay Hunt,
centre) and his friend Zeb (Otis Harlan). This
comedy revolves around the sale of their hotel on
the Nevada/California border and ran for two
years, which was unusual. Lazy Lightnin' (his
name is ironic) is another Ford outsider who is
proved right in the end, like Bim in 'Just Pals'.

RIGHT
Still from 'Hearts of Oak' (1924)
Sea captain Terry Dunnivan (Hobart Bosworth)
marries his young ward Chrystal (Pauline Starke).
When he finds out that her lost love is alive,
Dunnivan finds him before dying on a trip to the
Arctic. This is Ford's first sea film. A lost film.

ABOVE

Still from 'Kentucky Pride' (1925)

Jockey Little Mike, Jr. and groom/owner Mike Donovan (J. Farrell MacDonald, right) proudly parade the horses Virginia's Future and her daughter Confederacy after the latter's win. The film is narrated by Virginia's Future and, as Tag Gallagher points out, follows the Tradition and Duty theme that would become one of Ford's abiding themes in his later films.

LEFT

Still from 'The Fighting Heart' (1925)

Denny Bolton (George O'Brien) tries to live down his family's reputation as drunkards by becoming a prizefighter in New York. A lost film.

RIGHT
On the set of 'Thank You' (1925)
Alec Francis and John Ford.

BELOW
Still from 'Thank You' (1925)
Reverend David Lee (Alec Francis) comforts his
niece Diane (Jacqueline Logan). The gossip
spread around town harms them. In many of
Ford's films of this period, the priest, doctor,
judge or policeman are pillars of society who are
underappreciated. A lost film.

Still from 'The Shamrock Handicap' (1926)
The beginning of this film is set in a romanticised
Ireland, where the O'Haras have to sell all their
horses to pay off taxes. Then they sail to America
to make their fortune at horse racing.

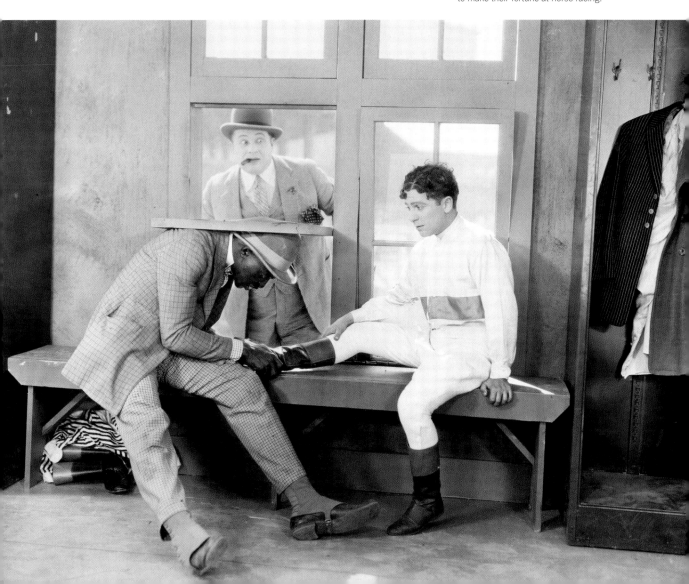

townspeople; when a gambler throws a drink in the face of a dance-hall girl she promptly pulls a derringer and shoots him. The movie has the stink of life, a sense of people in a landscape beyond any director working at the time.

Towns disappear and appear overnight as the population ceaselessly moves to the head of the track, but as the caravan moves on, a woman kneels at her husband's grave in the foreground. Ford bestows a sense of humanity onto all. When an Indian is shot in the course of an attack, a dog comes and lies down on its dead master. Ford is so confident of his story and theme that his handsome, muscular star (George O'Brien) doesn't make his entrance until the movie is 45 minutes old.

At the film's end, more than the tracks of the Union Pacific and the Central Pacific are united; an Italian labourer marries Nora Hogan and is congratulated by his Irish boss. One nation, one people. With *The Iron Horse*, Ford found his theme: a people triumphing over sectionalism and parochialism to stand together. It was Ford's first masterpiece, and the beginning of his claim to status as America's folk poet.

After *The Iron Horse*, many directors would have made a concerted effort to never make another programmer, but Ford went back to being a compliant contract director. He was a very skilled one, on the upper echelons of the studio system, but still more or less dependent on the quality of his scripts and cast. Sometimes his films had big stars, sometimes they barely had anybody you could legitimately call an actor. He was, in short, creatively erratic.

Hearts of Oak (1924) was a program picture; *Lightnin'* (1925) was a middling adaptation of a famous play of the period; *Kentucky Pride* (1925) was a horse picture, shameless and shamelessly sentimental; *The Fighting Heart* (1925) and *Thank You* (1925) more or less mid-range product of the period; *The Shamrock Handicap* (1926) was a follow-up to *Kentucky Pride*, and again effective.

Why was Ford wasting his professional time when he could have been capitalizing on his first stab of great success? He was in a contradictory psychological bind. On the one hand, his quixotic, evasive personality made him afraid to reveal anything about himself. On the other hand, artistry requires the expression of an inner personality. It would be years before Ford achieved sufficient self-confidence as a man and an artist to make the films he wanted to make, all of the time. At this point in his life, Ford may have been billing himself as John, but he remained a Jack of all directorial trades.

It was not until *3 Bad Men* (1926) that Ford returned to the large canvas, with the tale of a group of amiable reprobates who shepherd a young couple through the Oklahoma Land Rush. There are particularly beautiful locations in Jackson Hole, Wyoming (the land rush was shot in Victorville). It's a rich, compassionate picture in which all the girls, even a houseful of whores, are lovely.

In the end, the bad men (Tom Santschi, Ford regular J. Farrell MacDonald and Frank Campeau) sacrifice themselves for the young couple, i.e. the future – the first statement of a theme that Ford would return to again and again: sacrifices made to build a future that will never be as vital as the rough good times of the pioneer past. These dark characters are ghost riders on the horizon watching over the young family they died for – the future of the West.

Shortly after *3 Bad Men*, Ford's style underwent a radical transformation. *Mother Machree*, *Four Sons* and *Hangman's House* (all 1928) are all heavily under the influence of the great F. W. Murnau, whose *The Last Laugh* (1924) had been a

ABOVE
Publicity still for '3 Bad Men' (1926)
This is undoubtedly John Ford's best surviving silent Western. The eponymous 'bad' men are Spade Allen (Frank Campeau), Bull Stanley (Tom Santschi) and Mike Costigan (J. Farrell MacDonald).

OPPOSITE TOP
Still from '3 Bad Men' (1926)
When the 3 bad men see a wagon train heading West, they immediately pounce upon an opportunity to steal horses. However, instead of stealing from helpless Lee Carlton, they become her protectors. Although the affection that Bull has for Lee can be read as love, as the story develops we realise that Bull sees Lee as a substitute for his lost sister.

OPPOSITE BOTTOM
Still from '3 Bad Men' (1926)
The Reverend Calvin Benson (Alec B. Francis) is burnt out by the villainous Sheriff Layne Hunter and his men when they send flaming wagons down a hill into his shack. The Reverend's life is saved by Millie, Bull's sister, when she takes a bullet for him. Tragically, Bull is only reunited with her after she dies.

ABOVE
On the set of '3 Bad Men' (1926)
This picture was taken October 1925 on a dry lake in the Mojave Desert. From left are: "Joe" "The Greaser", Otis Harlan, Walter Perry, "Tony" "The Wop", "Nate" "The Hebe", George Harris, Duke Lee, John Stone (writer), Olive Borden, J. Farrell MacDonald, John Ford, Tom Santschi, Frank Campeau, Sol Wurtzel (general manager, Fox West Coast studios), George O'Brien and Louis Tellegen.

OPPOSITE TOP
Still from '3 Bad Men' (1926)
The climax of the film is the 1876 Dakota land rush. Ford captures the magnificent scale of the event.

OPPOSITE BOTTOM
Still from '3 Bad Men' (1926)
The settlers race for gold but in the process discover that the land itself is the real precious commodity.

ABOVE
Still from 'The Blue Eagle' (1926)
During World War One priest/skipper Joe (Robert
Edeson, centre) prevents Big Tim Ryan (William
Russell) and George Darcy (George O'Brien)
from fighting because there is a bigger fight for
them to win. After the war they continue to fight,
this time over a girl, but they eventually join
forces to defeat a drug smuggling ring. The
priest/skipper, a public figure with conflicting
duties, has his origins in Ford's father who, as
well as being a saloonkeeper (liquor was
prohibited in Maine), was an arbiter of justice
and a Democratic party ward boss. Other
examples of this figure are the
saloonkeeper/judge in 'The Iron Horse' and Ward
Bond's priest/Texas Ranger Captain Reverend
Samuel Clayton in 'The Searchers'.

RIGHT
Still from 'Upstream' (1927)
Gertie King (Nancy Nash) marries her knife-
throwing partner Jack LeVelle (Grant Withers),
although she loves actor Eric Brasingham. A lost
film.

ABOVE

Still from 'Mother Machree' (1928)
Ellen McHugh (Belle Bennett) receives news of
her fisherman husband's death from Father
MacShane (John MacSweeney). This
expressionistic opening sequence, set in Ireland,
is almost abstract. Ellen, called "Mother
Machree" ("Mother my heart") by her son Brian,
goes to America. Unable to find proper work,
Ellen becomes a sideshow entertainer and her
son is taken from her care. A lost film.

LEFT

Still from 'Mother Machree' (1928)
After working for many years as a housekeeper
for the wealthy Cutting family, Ellen (right) is
reunited with her son Brian (Neil Hamilton) when
Edith Cutting (Constance Howard) brings home
her new boyfriend. Ellen recognises her son
when he sings 'Mother Machree'. Ellen was the
first of Ford's great mother figures that continued
with 'Four Sons', 'Pilgrimage', 'The Grapes of
Wrath' and 'How Green Was My Valley'.

ABOVE
Still from 'Four Sons' (1928)
The opening scene presents a small German town as a kind of idyll, as Frau Bernle (Margaret Mann) does her washing. This film was heavily influenced by German Expressionist director F.W. Murnau. Not only did the camera move to follow the characters (as in Murnau's 'Der Letzte Mann' ('The Last Laugh', 1924)), but Ford used sets from Murnau's 'Sunrise' (1927), which was also filmed at the Fox studios.

RIGHT
Still from 'Four Sons' (1928)
Frau Bernle loses three of her sons in World War One. The fourth, Joseph Bernle (James Hall, left), goes to America and decides to fight for his new country because "everybody is equal." On the battlefield he hears a German soldier calling out to his mother (a chilling sound) and discovers it is his dying brother Andreas (George Meeker). At the end of the film, Frau Bernle goes to America to live with her son and his family.

revelation for serious Hollywood film-makers. When Murnau came to America to make *Sunrise* (1927) at Fox, he and Ford struck up a friendship, and Murnau wrote William Fox of his respect for his young colleague.

Ford's response was to endeavour to meld his own interests – family, community – with Murnau's style – stylized studio art direction and flowing tracking shots – the antithesis of the technique that Ford had been utilizing only a few years before. The student quickly became a master.

Mother Machree survives only in fragments, but it's visually impressive. It features some stunning lighting, with a deep chiaroscuro prefiguring the overtly artistic lighting schemes of *The Informer* (1935) and *The Long Voyage Home* (1940), as in a beautiful shot where a mother and son, unable to find a place to live because they're Irish, dejectedly descend a staircase in deep focus, moving away from the camera.

Four Sons is a long – perhaps too long – story of the price a German family pays for unthinking patriotism during World War One. But the masterpiece of this period is *Hangman's House*, a story of the Irish Troubles that constituted Ford's first full-scale immersion in the land of his ancestors. Enraptured by Murnau, Ford mounts long, lateral tracking shots that follow a hooded Victor McLaglen through studio sets representing Ireland – probably the redressed swamp set from *Sunrise*, which also saw use during *Four Sons*. The story isn't much – an IRA man returns home to kill the debauched Lord who married his sister and put her into an early grave – but the images are ravishing. Crumbling stone walls… Celtic crosses… the omnipresent Black and Tans – an effortless, poetic impression of an Ireland of the imagination. Add an exciting horse race, a jailbreak, and a fire that destroys the evil Lord as well as the house and its generational corruption and you have a completely memorable picture. "I'm going back to the brown desert," says Victor McLaglen's Citizen Hogan in farewell, "but I'm taking the green place with me in my heart."

Hangman's House is as polished a piece of UFA worship as anything in American cinema but, even though it contains rough blueprints for both *The Informer* and *The Quiet Man* (1952), it lacks the warmth and humour that Ford's work had displayed as early as 1917. Ford would get that back, but it would take a few years.

Still from 'Hangman's House' (1928)
Dermott McDermott (Larry Kent, centre) and Citizen Hogan (Victor McLaglen, right) confront scoundrel John D'Arcy (Earle Foxe). D'Arcy plotted to win the hand (and estates) of Dermott's sweetheart, and Hogan's sister died after D'Arcy abandoned her.

Lost and Found
1928–1941

Ford had experimented with sound as early as *Four Sons*, notably a striking battlefield scene, as one of the sons, now wounded, cries out for his mother. The disembodied cries of "Mütterchen" are genuinely eerie; even a plaintive clarinet from the orchestra in the pit wouldn't have been half so effective as a few words moaned at the appropriate emotional point.

Another early attempt, which features extensive sound effects but no actual dialogue, is a comedy called *Riley the Cop* (1928), a vehicle for the character actor and Ford regular J. Farrell MacDonald. It's a pleasant time-passer in which MacDonald travels to Munich to extradite a suspect. It starts out as a mild little comedy-drama that turns into a supposedly rollicking fish-out-of-water comedy, with the relaxed Irishman butting heads with the authoritarian Germans. Result: alcoholic hijinks and much cultural confusion.

Ford's broad Irish humour is an indispensable seasoning, but insufficiently varied to sustain an entire film all by itself. *Riley the Cop* would be of little interest if it weren't for the soundtrack, which never shuts up. Children yell, yodellers yodel, bats hit balls with a loud crack, windows break, people laugh, the crowd at a beer garden joins in song. No opportunity to match a sound effect with an on-screen action is passed up.

Ford's first all-talking picture was a short entitled *Napoleon's Barber* (1928), now lost. In the latter part of 1928, the sound panic was hitting Hollywood, and Ford had no choice except to go along. Not that it would ever change his primary loyalty. "I... am a silent picture man," he would say as an old man. "Pictures, not words, should tell the story."

Sound streamlined Ford's style – rarely would there be the luxuriant tracking shots found in *Hangman's House*, for instance – but it also flattened it. Ford's ambition seemed to decline, as he compliantly took more or less whatever Fox gave him. In the early days of sound, Fox was a severely damaged organization because of William Fox's financial over-extension and the disaster wrought by the stock market crash at a time when he could least afford it.

The Black Watch (1929), an adaptation of Talbot Mundy's *King of the Khyber Rifles*, is a good example of the obstacles directors had to cope with in sound. The film looks exquisite – the cameraman was the great Joe August – and the sound recording is first rate, but the proceedings tend to come to a regular halt for one thing or another. There is silent film atmosphere infected by clumsy dialogue, with

On the set of 'Wee Willie Winkie' (1937)
Ford tries to get his script back from Anna May, veteran movie elephant. In reality Ford didn't need it. He memorised the complete script and the images he wanted before filming began.

"He has taken an enormously distinguished artistic career absolutely for granted. He has the artistic point of view of an old Renaissance craftsman. He just could do it, without a lot of conversation."

Katharine Hepburn

Still from 'Napoleon's Barber' (1928)
This short film was Ford's first all-talking film. A barber brags to his client what he would do to Napoleon (Otto Matieson, on horse), unaware that Napoleon is under his blade. During filming Ford told the sound man to record a coach going over a bridge. The sound man argued that it would not work, but it did, and became perhaps the first use of location sound in a dramatic film. A lost film.

the actors taking lllllloooooonnnngggg pauses between lines, to let the audience savour the full import. There are also endless shots of troops marching and pipers piping just to put across the unaccustomed thrill of sound.

That was followed by a film about Annapolis called *Salute* (1929), which goes *The Black Watch* one better by offering indifferent camerawork and bad acting. Ford's first batch of talkies weren't impressive, but they were better than the first talkies of other top-rank silent directors such as Fred Niblo or James Cruze.

Ford began to find his rhythm with *Men Without Women* (1930), a resolutely compelling submarine picture that falters only when compared to Frank Capra's *Submarine* (1928), which undoubtedly served as its inspiration. *Men Without Women* is an unusually coarse film for Ford – at one point, sailors negotiate prices with Shanghai whores. It's a patchy early talkie, but it also has echoes of better days ahead – a religious fanatic who goes crazy, like Boris Karloff in *The Lost Patrol* (1934), and an Englishman with a poignant secret, as with Ian Hunter in *The Long Voyage Home*.

Born Reckless (1930) is a minor gem, a genial gangster movie in the vein of Sternberg's *Underworld* (1927). *Up The River* (1930) was a programmer, and *Seas Beneath* (1931) is a return to the ocean that Ford loved, with Catalina standing in for the Canary Islands.

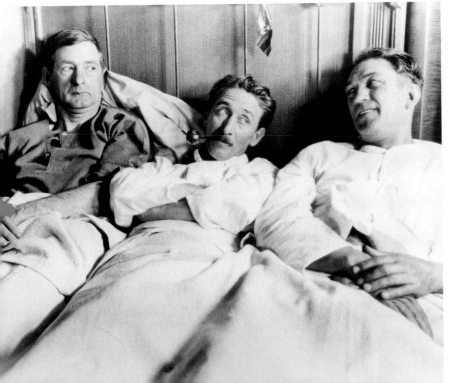

ABOVE
Still from 'Riley the Cop' (1928)
Soft-hearted cop Aloysius Riley (J. Farrell MacDonald, in top hat) travels to Munich, Germany and collects Davy Collins (David Rollins, right) to question him about a missing $5,000. However, the beer and beermaids get the better of Riley and Davy has to drag Riley back to America.

LEFT
Still from 'Strong Boy' (1929)
Slim (Slim Summerville), Pete (Clyde Cook) and William "Strong Boy" Bloss (Victor McLaglen) are railroad porters in this humorous story. Whilst filming at a railroad station, the Western Controller of Traffic threw out the crew. Ford spent four days building a station set in a studio before he found out that McLaglen had played a practical joke on him. Ford said nothing. Some time later, whilst boarding a train to Mexico, McLaglen was stopped by officials. Without suitable I.D. McLaglen was dragged off, sobbing, and fed bread and water in a cell before Ford let him off the hook. A lost film.

ABOVE
Still from 'Salute' (1929)
Ineffectual Paul Randall (William Janney, top centre) enters Annapolis to train for the Navy, following the great tradition of his family. His brother John (George O'Brien), who is training for the Army at West Point, believes that "if you want anything, you've got to grab it." Paul thinks he wants flighty Marion Wilson (Joyce Compton, right) but he eventually realises that charming Nancy Wayne (Helen Chandler, left) is the girl for him. This swimming competition scene was not included in the film.

RIGHT
Still from 'The Black Watch' (1929)
Tradition and duty play a major part in this film. The tradition of the Black Watch, a Scottish regiment, is shown through their rituals. It is Captain Donald King's duty to abandon his regiment on the eve of their departure to World War One and to seduce Yasmani (Myrna Loy), a goddess leading an Afghan hill tribe. When she bids them to stop, she is killed.

The Brat (1931), a variation on *Pygmalion*, is the worst picture Ford ever made. After an arty, expressionist first reel, the film declines into orthodoxy, a photographed play with slapdash production – in one rear-projected sequence of an ambulance racing past theatres, the film is projected the wrong way and all the letters on the marquees are backwards. Except for Ward Bond and J. Farrell MacDonald lurking around the scenes, there is no indication that John Ford was anywhere in the vicinity.

Then he was lent out to Samuel Goldwyn to direct *Arrowsmith* (1931), a well-wrought adaptation of the Sinclair Lewis novel. *Arrowsmith* – about the conflict between a doctor's idealism and the real world – is too didactic and metaphorical to be of complete interest to Ford (King Vidor would have been a better choice) but Ford took the visual possibilities and ran with them. Richard Day's expressionist sets are continually impressive, but Ford only cuts loose in the picture's final third, when Martin Arrowsmith and his wife move to the West Indies to stem an epidemic of plague. The sets shift from high ceilings and the deco lines of the city to low ceilings, wide-planked floors, latticed doors, and an omnipresent, unhealthy-looking mist that floats through the sets. The sequence is a sustained *tour de force* of voodoo Gothic.

After that, it was back to jobs of work, with *Air Mail* (1932) – mainly of interest because it's clearly the inspiration for Howard Hawks' *Only Angels Have Wings* (1939) – and *Flesh* (1932), a wrestling picture with Wallace Beery that seems to be the premise for the movie that Barton Fink is attempting to write in the Coen brothers' uproarious movie of the same name. But neither John Ford nor Barton Fink could do much with a Wallace Beery wrestling movie.

As it had been in the silents, so it was in the talkies; Ford was consistently inconsistent, alternating pictures of authentic accomplishment with time-passers where he barely bothered to show up. At this point, he was on track toward a career analogous to someone like Victor Fleming or Henry King – a first-rate studio director, but an essentially reactive talent.

Ford was clearly treading water, but help arrived just in time, with the superb *Pilgrimage* (1933). It was a film that came and went quickly, but seen today it is an audacious effort worthy of Henry James. It's the story of Hannah Jessop, a mean, Bible-thumping widow in Arkansas in 1918. Trying to keep her son from a woman she doesn't like, she gets the boy drafted, in spite of the fact his girlfriend is pregnant. Her son is killed in World War One, and she spends the next ten years spurning her grandson's overtures. Ten years after the death of her son, Hannah goes with a group of other mothers to visit their sons' graves in France. Her experiences during her pilgrimage transform a purebred provincial bitch into a human being.

Ford manages to avoid the obvious pitfalls of the story. Working almost completely in the studio, creating atmospherics that recall *Hangman's House*, Ford makes a virtue out of what in lesser hands would be claustrophobic. The story is worthy of Griffith at his best, and Ford steers the cast into uninsistent, naturalistic acting that lifts the movie above melodrama. Hannah is a fierce old woman who could be the elderly daughter of Ethan Edwards – determined, bitter, unforgiving. But the experience of Europe gives her experiences that promote growth. From intolerance there is the beginning of wisdom, the beginnings of a live-and-let-live beneficence. And in the performance of the unheralded Henrietta Crosman, Ford reveals a skill with actresses that he had previously kept hidden. It's the finest character actress performance in any Ford film, including Jane Darwell in *The Grapes of Wrath*.

ABOVE
Still from 'Men Without Women' (1930)
Cobb (Walter McGrail) sets up virgin Pollosk (George LeGuere) with a girl.

OPPOSITE TOP
Still from 'Men Without Women' (1930)
The film begins with an extended sequence in Shanghai at 'the longest bar in the world'. The men indulge in a lot of singing and drinking as part of the male bonding ritual.

OPPOSITE BOTTOM
Still from 'Men Without Women' (1930)
The early Harry Carey Westerns dealt with self-sacrifice, duty and moral issues. In films like '3 Bad Men' and 'The Blue Eagle,' Ford developed these ideas in stories about male groups under pressure. The tension element was raised in 'Men Without Women' and 'The Lost Patrol' before Ford went on to explore the dynamics of the family and community in later films. In this scene the men begin to crack under the pressure.

PAGES 76/77
On the set of 'Men Without Women' (1930)
Actors Walter McGrail, J. Farrell MacDonald and Kenneth MacKenna chat while Ford (seated) talks to cinematographer Joseph H. August (with cigarette behind his ear).

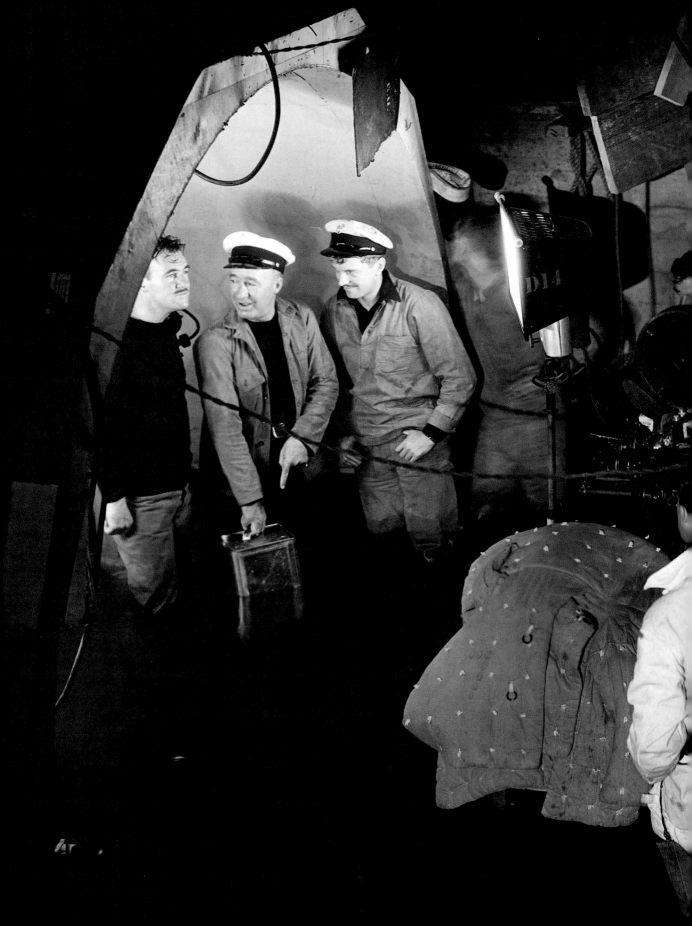

Still from 'Born Reckless' (1930)
A District Attorney sends three criminals to World War One rather than to jail. The leader Louis Beretti (Edmund Lowe) takes advantage of the situation and French girl (Yola D'Avril) in this comedic Army sequence. When they return to New York, this messy film changes into a gangster melodrama.

Looking to extend his reach and make some more personal pictures, Ford struck a two-picture deal with Merian C. Cooper at RKO. Cooper was a high-energy adventurer who, with his partner Ernest Schoedsack, had made such landmark ethnographic epics as *Grass* (1925) and *Chang* (1927), before transitioning to high adventure with *The Four Feathers* (1929) and the epic fantasy *King Kong* (1933). Cooper had taken over as production chief at RKO after David O. Selznick left for MGM, and he was a Ford fan. The two men struck a deal that involved two pictures that the two men would mutually agree on, and a low fee – $15,000 apiece – against 12 1/2 percent of the gross after each picture earned back double its negative cost. Ford leaped at the deal, and just like that had formed a partnership with a man who would prove to be every bit as crucial a collaborator as John Wayne.

The first of the two pictures was *The Lost Patrol*, made in a tight 21 days on location outside Yuma, Arizona. The setting is Mesopotamia during World War One; a British patrol is set upon by a band of unseen Arabs who pick off the soldiers one by one, until only Victor McLaglen is left alive.

The British die when they do the wrong thing, but they also die when they do the right thing. The picture is tense, dramatic and believable. Ford errs only in

Still from 'Seas Beneath' (1931)
John Ford loved the sea and returned to it time and again as a background or film subject: 'Hearts of Oak' (1924), 'The Blue Eagle' (1926), 'Salute' (1929), 'Men Without Women' (1930), 'Seas Beneath' (1931), 'Submarine Patrol' (1938), 'The Long Voyage Home' (1940), 'They Were Expendable' (1945), 'Mister Roberts' (1955) and 'The Wings of Eagles' (1957).

allowing Boris Karloff, playing a religious fanatic, to plunge deeply into hysteria from his very first scene, which gives him no room to build. There is too much Karloff, and a little too much Max Steiner, although the composer does pull off a notable *coup de théâtre* when he uses a wordless, moaning chorus that eerily underscores the patrol's isolation as the night closes in. *The Lost Patrol* stands firm today – lean, concise, achieving its melodramatic effects with ease and economy.

One step forward, two steps back. Ford returned to Fox to direct *The World Moves On* (1934), a mushy multi-generational saga that moves from 1825 to 1929, with Franchot Tone and Madeleine Carroll gazing soulfully at each other over teacups. The film is enlivened only by the unlikely appearance of Stepin Fetchit in the French army, which sends the otherwise sober film sky-high. The world moves on, but not nearly fast enough.

A sidetrip over to Columbia to direct *The Whole Town's Talking* (1935), a mildly charming Edward G. Robinson vehicle, didn't ultimately seem worth the effort either.

Ford began to split his time between two very different studios and developed two very specific artistic personalities. Fox was for homespun entertainment, while RKO would represent artistic experimentation. Without the long leash granted him by Darryl Zanuck, who took over Fox in 1935, it's entirely possible that Ford

Still from 'Seas Beneath' (1931)
Captain Bob (George O'Brien) is running a Q-boat, a schooner that hunts German submarines by acting as a decoy. However, the schooner has a cannon on board and a US submarine trailing it for protection.

wouldn't have developed a sufficient fluency with his high-art style to enable him, in movies like *The Grapes of Wrath* (1940) and *My Darling Clementine* (1946), to synthesize both aspects of his creative personality into a seamless whole.

At Fox, Ford was fortuitously teamed with Will Rogers. Ford and Rogers would make three pictures in three years, and would undoubtedly have made many more if Rogers hadn't been killed in a plane crash in 1935. Both men had developed a specialty in bucolic truths, and it was quickly apparent that they brought out the best in each other. Rogers was the quintessential rural American personality, with a winning, if slightly one-note, aw-shucks persona. Ford deepened that, and filled in some of the lazier cracks in Rogers' character with intimations of loss and genuine moments of regret. Ford's gift for depicting a community – in the case of the Rogers films, an insular, slightly petty one – gave Rogers' character a reason for his gentle disillusion.

For Ford, Rogers was akin to Harry Carey, an unassuming, unpretentious man who never had to raise his voice to make people listen. The first of their collaborations, *Doctor Bull* (1933), involves a country doctor who inoculates children against typhoid fever in spite of the fears of his town. At the end, sick of hypocrisy, he and his lady friend depart the town for a better life, rather like unmelodramatic versions of Gary Cooper and Grace Kelly in *High Noon* (1952).

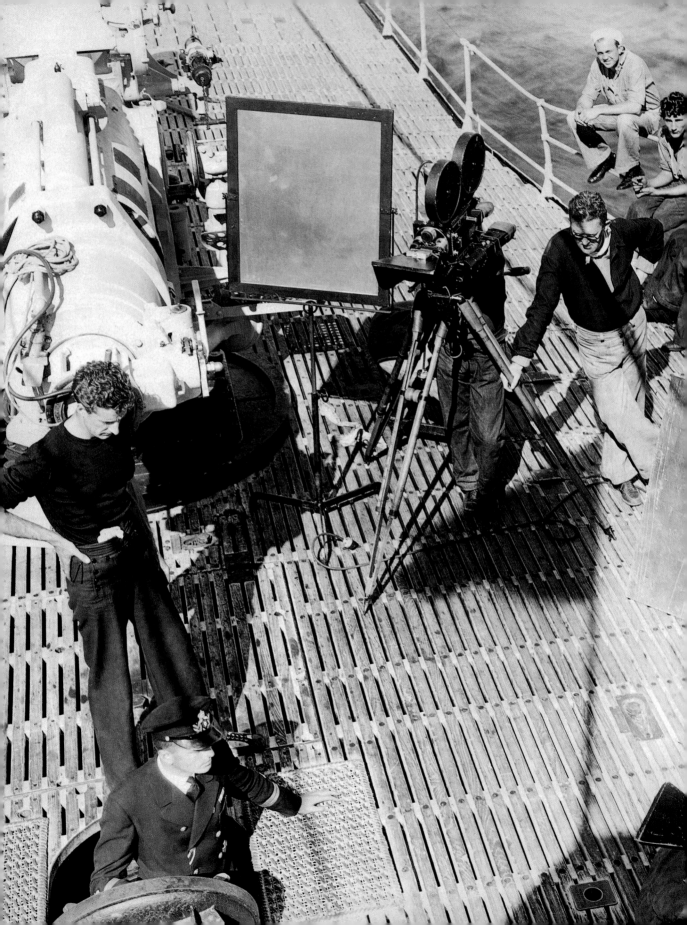

"He was really a genius. He'd listen, but if you were smart, you'd spend a lot of time listening to him. He knew more about photography than any man who ever worked in the movies. He'd force me into situations where I'd have to sit up and take notice."

William H. Clothier

ABOVE
Still from 'Seas Beneath' (1931)
The realistic and stunning photography of Joseph H. August gave credence to a sometimes silly plot.

LEFT
On the set of 'Seas Beneath' (1931)
John Ford (right of camera) oversees filming on the world's biggest submarine, the 'USS V-4'. Ford portrayed the Navy and the other armed services in a positive light throughout his career and so was able to secure a high degree of cooperation from them.

ABOVE
Still from 'The Brat' (1931)
A poor girl (Sally O'Neill) cannot pay for her meal, so the judge orders her to stay with writer MacMillan Forester, so that he can research 'a rose in the gutter.' Here she does some research of her own and reads his book 'The Restless Virgin'.

RIGHT
Still from 'The Brat' (1931)
After MacMillan makes passes at her, the brat rejects him and makes her own passes at MacMillan's drunk brother Stephen (Frank Albertson).

"Anybody can direct a picture once they know the fundamentals. Directing is not a mystery, it's not an art. The main thing about directing is: photograph the people's eyes."

John Ford

Judge Priest (1934) is the story of Billy Priest, who takes people as they are, whether the law approves or not. "The name of Priest means something in Kentucky!" thunders his frosty sister-in-law. "I never heard it meant intolerance," he replies.

Ford sets the film up as a classic confrontation between propriety and the natural man without whom the perilously maintained order of things collapses. *Judge Priest* is a film of remembrance and longing; Billy Priest leans back and puts his feet up (just like Henry Fonda in *My Darling Clementine*), plays godfather to young lovers, does call and response with Hattie McDaniel, and lights a candle by his dead wife's picture, his own sorrowing image reflected in the glass. He also goes to the cemetery to fill her in on current events, the first appearance of what would be among Ford's most heartfelt, moving moments. For Ford, death ended a life, not a relationship.

Steamboat Round the Bend (1935) is probably the least of the three pictures. Rogers again is playing a Confederate veteran, now selling patent medicines from his riverboat. Both the ship and its owner are genially unkempt and disreputable, which to Ford meant authenticity. The film is mostly about class distinctions, which Americans like to believe they're above. Ford knew better. As always with Ford, the defining unit is not the individual, but the family.

Still from 'Arrowsmith' (1931)
Doctor Martin Arrowsmith is a driven man. He invests himself completely in the glory of medical research, and is supported by his selfless wife Leora (Helen Hayes). Unfortunately, in his haste to prove the effectiveness of his serum on West Indian natives, he accidently releases a plague virus that ultimately kills his wife. Despite his sorrow, and the glory he attains with his serum, we are left with the impression that Arrowsmith has not learned to be human, but is just as driven at the end as he was in the beginning.

Still from 'Air Mail' (1932)
Duke (Pat O'Brien, left) rescues crashed friend Mike (Ralph Bellamy) by landing in a dangerously narrow canyon. The air is full of machismo in another film that praises driven antiheroes. These are the antecedents of the glory-seeking Colonel Thursby in 'Fort Apache' and the racist rescuer/revenger Ethan Edwards in 'The Searchers'.

Will Rogers died in August 1935; years later, Ford was asked what the men of the West were really like. "They were like Will Rogers," he said simply.

For the second of the two pictures for Merian C. Cooper and RKO, the choice was *The Informer* (1935), based on Liam O'Flaherty's short novel. Ford approached production carefully; he and Dudley Nichols wrote the script together on a cruise to Mexico and back. When they returned, there were rumours around town that RKO was going to slot their dutiful but dull leading man Richard Dix into the title role, but Ford made sure that Victor McLaglen got the part.

The Informer was shot quickly, because there wasn't enough money to shoot it any other way. Ford was in his element, working fast but with a great deal of freedom and a handpicked cast. True, the actors were something of a mishmash; the only authentic Irishman in the cast was J. M. Kerrigan, playing the wheedling toady who helps Gypo squander his 20 pounds of blood money.

"The crew knew what he wanted as much as he did," actor and later Ford friend Robert Parrish remembered. "They knew he didn't want big camera movement and didn't want standard close-ups. He had a thing about the eyes. 'Look in people's

Still from 'Flesh' (1932)
Wrestler Polakai (Wallace Beery, centre) wins
another match. He falls heavily for a girl, and
marries her, only to find out that she is using
him. Beery is a loveable oaf of a type often found
in Ford's movies, usually played by Victor
McLaglen.

eyes, see what they're telling you,' he said. He would talk about the lighting. There
was a shot of a street-singer, and Ford came up to Joe August. 'You got any
shadows? Paste one on the back wall there, will you?'"

The RKO brass may not have believed in the picture, but the critics fell on it with
expressions of rapture. *The Nation* referred to its 'superb direction'. The *National
Board of Review* magazine noted the picture's 'grim splendor.' *The Informer* became
a sleeper hit. Produced for $243,000 – cheap, but not outrageously cheap – it grossed
$891,000 worldwide, for a net profit of $290,000. *The Informer* won McLaglen the
Best Actor Oscar, and after directing pictures for 20 years, Ford won his first
Academy Award for Direction, firmly establishing him with high-brow critics and
audiences. As an example of how modest his European profile had been, the 1938
History of Motion Pictures by Bardèche and Brasillach hailed Ford as a clever and
dependable 'newcomer' on the basis of *The Lost Patrol, The Informer* and a few
other pictures.

The proletarian theme and overt symbolism of the film have caused its reputation
to decline in recent years – one generation's shattering masterpiece is another

Still from 'Pilgrimage' (1933)

Hannah Jessop (Henrietta Crosman) is a domineering and jealous mother who sends her son to die in World War One rather than let him marry the girl he loves. After his death, she puts together a photo of her son she had torn up. This is one of Ford's rare films where the mother is the force that destroys the family rather than keep it together.

generation's threadbare warhorse. The film's heavy dramaturgy and rampant Catholicism give it a rhetorical quality out of key with the evolution of Ford's career and make it seem a trifle stifling.

Yet *The Informer* retains a good deal of the compressed, allegorical power of one long, grim night in Dublin. Many of the film's excesses derive directly from Liam O'Flaherty's novel, and some of its most touching moments, as when Katie tells Gypo, "I'll love you when I'm clay," are not in the book at all. And always, there is McLaglen's Gypo, in all his bruised, brutish humanity – so stupid, so uneasy in his own skin, failing at being a rebel, failing at being an informer.

After the breakthrough of *The Informer*, Ford went back into his sporadic mode. *The Prisoner of Shark Island* (1936) was a first-rate film about Dr. Samuel Mudd, the man who set the broken leg of John Wilkes Booth, apparently without knowing he had killed Lincoln, and was sent to Devil's Island for doing what a doctor is supposed to do. Although saddled with the unsympathetic Warner Baxter as a leading man, Ford resonated to the combination of American history and personal anguish; the film is continually impressive visually, and marked the last time Ford and Harry Carey would work together.

But that was followed by *Mary of Scotland* (1936), a top-heavy costume spectacle whose sole distinction was its introduction of Katharine Hepburn into Ford's life.

Still from 'Doctor Bull' (1933)
Doctor George Bull (Will Rogers), attends to
Virginia Banning (Rochelle Hudson) but she
needs more than medical attention. Bull rings
her boyfriend and arranges for them to be
together, even pretending to be Virginia's mother.
Bull's skill is not just medical. He has a common
sense approach to life, love and happiness that
punctures the hypocrisy of the townspeople he
helps.

The two began a serious affair that was the only time Ford's marriage was
imperilled. Ultimately, he refused to leave his wife, and Hepburn moved on to
another married, alcoholic Irishman named Spencer Tracy.

A return to Ireland came to nought as Ford's version of Sean O'Casey's *The
Plough and the Stars* (1936) was heavily re-edited by the studio. The released version
ran a ridiculously brief 67 minutes, proving that the prestige success of *The Informer*
only extended so far. In spite of its crashing failure, Ford had no intention of
swearing off Irish subjects; the same year he came a cropper with *The Plough and the
Stars*, he optioned a story by Maurice Walsh that he had read in *The Saturday
Evening Post*, about a boxer who returns to Ireland and falls in love with a delightful
colleen. It was called 'The Quiet Man'.

Seeking to bolster his commercial bona fides, Ford directed Shirley Temple in
Wee Willie Winkie (1937), and made a good, if not distinguished film that capitalized
on the enormous size differential between Shirley Temple and Victor McLaglen. It's
vividly directed, with a beautifully orchestrated build-up to a battle that doesn't
happen because two wise warriors keep their heads and make peace – the same
dynamic that makes the climax of *She Wore a Yellow Ribbon* (1949) so unexpected.
And there is a restrained, genuinely touching death scene for Victor McLaglen,
which gives a human scale to the imperialist derring-do.

ABOVE
Still from 'The Lost Patrol' (1934)
At the end of the ordeal at a lonely oasis, the Sergeant (Victor McLaglen) is the only survivor, although he has been driven half mad. The graves of his comrades are marked with gleaming swords in a typical Fordian gesture of self-sacrifice.

LEFT
On the set of 'The Lost Patrol' (1934)
Victor McLaglen and Douglas Walton stand on boxes so that director Ford (sitting at left) can get the angle he wants.

ABOVE
Still from 'The World Moves On' (1934)
Robert Girard (Franchot Tone, right duellist)
defends the honour of Mary Warburton. He wins,
but must vow never to marry her. Set between
1824 and 1929, this film follows the Girard and
Warburton families over several generations of
tradition and duty as that vow is kept.

RIGHT
Still from 'The Whole Town's Talking' (1935)
Arthur Ferguson Jones (Edward G. Robinson,
left) is a timid clerk who finds out that he
resembles gangster Killer Mannion (Edward G.
Robinson, right) in this fast-moving screwball
comedy. Mannion uses Jones' likeness to his
advantage, switching roles so that he can carry
out a murder. But the pendulum swings both
ways when Mannion's gang think that Jones is
their leader. (Note the double exposure on the
typewriter, probably caused because the eyeline
needed to be matched.)

Then it was back to the Goldwyn studio for *The Hurricane* (1937), a well-mounted South Sea spectacle, where Ford again ran afoul of the producer's penchant for control. Specifically, Goldwyn had promised to let Ford do some location shooting in the South Seas, then reneged. Ford was furious.

Nevertheless, *The Hurricane* emerged as a South Sea idyll in the tradition of Robert J. Flaherty's *Moana* (1926) or W. S. Van Dyke's *White Shadows in the South Seas* (1928) – the white man's depredations visited on the innocent children of the sun in French Polynesia, with an elaborate storm sequence Ford must have adored shooting. (He rarely used second units, and almost always shot his own action.)

For Ford, it was something of a return to the silent days, and it's among the most sensual of his films. The set-up is verbal, but after that there are long stretches of the film that are entirely visual – a lovely sequence of a marriage feast followed by a wedding night, or a lengthy, rather expressionist montage involving Jon Hall's attempted escape from prison. Pictures, mood and rhythm were always Ford's supreme gifts.

While Ford was enjoying his status as one of Hollywood's top film-makers, he was still clearly hungry for more. He had found a kindred spirit in Merian C. Cooper, and the two men began mulling the possibilities of independent production. At this point, the problem for film-makers wanting to leave the tight embrace of the

Still from 'Judge Priest' (1934)
In a moving scene, Judge Priest (Will Rogers, right) talks to his departed wife and children at their graveside. When he sees Bob Gillis (David Landau) place flowers on the grave of Ellie May Gillespie's mother, Judge Priest realises Gillis is Ellie May's father. The easy-going humanity of Judge Priest made this film the one of 1934's top grossing movies.

studios involved both access to finance – the biggest stars, who might be said to constitute collateral for the loans, were tied up in exclusive contracts to studios and would not be lent out for anything approaching independent competition – and access to theatres. The studios controlled the vast majority of the theatres in America, and, naturally enough, looked with disfavour on promoting competition to their own way of doing things. United Artists, the friendliest company for independent producers, had very few theatres of their own.

Nevertheless, in mid-1937, the trade papers announced the formation of Renowned Artists, a group to include Ford and Tay Garnett. Renowned Artists fell through, but Ford and Cooper didn't give up. They chose as their company logo a silhouette of a three-masted sailing ship, and they called their company Argosy.

Ford had perfected a method of making pictures that made the industrial nature of movie-making seem as effortless as possible. In essence, Ford carried the completed picture in his head and shot the movie to match the one in his head. He determined in advance what every scene should look like, what lines should be played in a medium shot, which in close-up, and he shot the picture so it could only be cut that way. He did not play each scene through in a master shot, then play the same scene in over-the-shoulder close-ups, but rather shot only the part of the master and the close-ups that he intended to be used.

Added to that was his penchant for shooting only a couple of takes. Daily shooting reports indicate that Ford shot only one take between 30 and 40 percent of the time, and the bulk of the work was completed in two or three takes.

All this meant that production time was minimized; a Ford film habitually came in under schedule and on budget, although his penchant for location shooting meant that occasionally time would be lost to bad weather. A Ford film gave the studio less film to play with, and they couldn't really re-edit it without re-shooting, but that seemed like a fair exchange for the saving of money.

Ford was not the only director to shoot like this – Alfred Hitchcock was famous for it, although he sometimes used storyboards and sketches so that his technical people could keep his picture continuity straight, but Ford and MGM's W. S. Van Dyke II kept it all in their mind.

1938 brought nothing special: *Four Men and a Prayer* and *Submarine Patrol*. But Ford was gathering his energies and was about to launch into the most sustained burst of creativity any director has ever had. Between 1939 and 1941, he would direct seven films. All of the films were about families, either actual or *ad hoc* – families imperilled, families destroyed, families holding together. Four would be masterpieces (*Stagecoach, Young Mr. Lincoln, The Grapes of Wrath, How Green Was My Valley*). Two would be merely excellent (*Drums Along the Mohawk* and *The Long Voyage Home*). Only *Tobacco Road* would be a quickly forgotten failure. But the great critical and commercial success of the majority of the films, and two consecutive Best Director Oscars (for *Grapes of Wrath* and *How Green Was My Valley*) would put Ford firmly on the top rung of American directors, where he would remain for the rest of his career.

Stagecoach (1939) introduced two primary elements into the Ford universe: John Wayne and Monument Valley. Ford had known John Wayne since his name was Marion Morrison. In 1928, Morrison was in pre-law at USC and playing football when he got a summer job as an assistant prop man at Fox. One day during the production of *Four Sons*, an absent-minded Morrison, carrying a broom, walked

ABOVE
Still from 'The Informer' (1935)
This morality play shows how idealism can fall prey to human weakness. Gypo Nolan (Victor McLaglen) is a simple Irish brute, who informs on his best friend and comrade-in-arms Frankie McPhillip for money, so that he and his girlfriend can sail to a new life in America. Gypo is shot by the IRA and escapes to a church, where he asks forgiveness of Frankie's mother (Una O'Connor) before dying.

OPPOSITE
On the set of 'The Informer' (1935)
John Ford watches as Katie Madden (Margo Grahame) comforts her boyfriend Gypo. Ford got a drunken performance from Victor McLaglen by making sure that McLaglen was inebriated. McLaglen won an Academy Award.

ABOVE
Still from 'Steamboat Round the Bend' (1935)
Each of the characters in this rambling tale
undergoes a change of identity or profession.
Here Doctor John Pearly (Will Rogers, left)
changes the identities of the wax figures so that
the museum will appeal to a Southern audience.
Efe (Francis Ford), the drunk/steamboat
engineer helps out. Francis Ford appeared in 30
of his brother's films, often playing a drunken
fool character.

RIGHT
Still from 'Steamboat Round the Bend' (1935)
The race against the clock to save Duke (John
McGuire) from the hangman is reminiscent of
the framing sequence in D.W. Griffith's
'Intolerance' (1916). Except here, it is literally a
race, only with steamboats.

On the set of 'The Prisoner of Shark Island' (1936)
This set still is poignant because Harry Carey plays his last role for Ford, as the Commandant of Fort Jefferson aka "Shark Island".

onto a set while Ford was rolling his cameras. Astonished and delighted, Ford just sat there enjoying the moment, waiting to see what Morrison's reaction would be. Eventually, the young football player looked up, saw the cameraman cranking and realized what he had done. Morrison threw down his broom and, undoubtedly expecting to be fired, began running off the stage. Ford called him back, pinned a prop medal on him, kicked him in the backside and told him to get out. But he didn't fire him.

It was the beginning of one of the most productive relationships of Ford's life. He took the big, good-natured boy under his wing and made him a member of the Ford crew. Morrison, whose own father was a feckless, henpecked druggist, responded to Ford's quiet strength and aura of power. The fact that Ford knew and understood football helped too.

Morrison can be seen in a prominent bit in *Hangman's House*, as an over-enthusiastic spectator at a steeplechase. He did some stuntwork and played other small parts, and became such a presence around the Fox lot that he was re-christened John Wayne and picked as the star of Raoul Walsh's lavish 1930 Western failure *The Big Trail*. After that, it was B-Westerns for eight long years.

"I would rather have been in the Ford Stock Company than be a star. There was no way to become a star, but you felt good about your craft. He was a wonderful man in every way. I loved him."

Anna Lee

98

ABOVE
Still from 'Mary of Scotland' (1936)
Mary Stuart (Katharine Hepburn) with her devoted secretary and confidant David Rizzio (John Carradine).

LEFT
Production sketch for 'Mary of Scotland' (1936)
This production sketch is for the above scene.

*"John was a lovely person, but he had his quirks.
He would never look through the camera, and he
would never interfere with the lighting. He would
say, 'Shoot it from here,' indicating with his hand,
standing on the studio floor looking at the set. He
hated panning and tracking, anything like that. He
wanted the actors to play to the camera, move
within the composition."*

Freddie Young

Ford and Wayne stayed friendly, but Wayne had begun to despair of ever getting
out of the B-Western ghetto. When Ford bought the rights to *Stagecoach*, he was
determined that the part of the Ringo Kid would go to John Wayne, even though
everybody else in the business felt him to be damaged goods. Wouldn't Gary
Cooper be a much better idea? How about Joel McCrea?

Technically, *Stagecoach* was produced by Walter Wanger, but Wanger was well-
known in the industry for being a comparatively hands-off producer who gave his
directors a good deal of autonomy. Wanger let Ford have his way about Wayne and
everything else, including the script, which Ford fashioned with Dudley Nichols. It
would probably be wise to regard *Stagecoach* as the first production of Argosy Pictures.

As for Monument Valley, it was not exactly unknown to civilization – the
Western author Zane Grey passed through in 1913, and there are brief glimpses of
the valley in George B. Seitz's *The Vanishing American* (1925). But the inaccessibility
of Monument Valley worked against any widespread use of the location.

Ford told his grandson Dan that it was George O'Brien who told him about the
Valley; a variant version is that Harry Goulding, who owned a trading post in the
Valley, heard that there was a Western called *Stagecoach* being planned for the
Flagstaff area. Goulding packed up a bunch of stills of Monument Valley and drove
all the way to Los Angeles to present them to the staff at Walter Wanger
Productions. Wanger wasn't there, but Ford was, and when he saw the stills, he told
Goulding, "I'd always wanted to do a picture up there."

When he first examined the Valley's 96,000 acres, Ford found the ultimate frame
for his pictures: sandstone buttes punching through the earth's crusts like fists, as
well as delicate architectural spires rising toward the sky. It is a place of majesty and
repose, and it gives the impression that it is as it has always been – permanent,
implacable and sacred.

At night, clouds descend and settle over the buttes and pillars like gods visiting
their creation. Even the watchful, uncommunicative Navajo must have appealed to
Ford as kindred spirits. This was not Newhall, not even Lone Pine, this was *out there*

– a full 180 miles from the nearest railroad, with an endless series of compositional possibilities. Here, finally, were the mountains to match the men Ford could put on the screen.

In the years to come, Ford would ritualistically return to Monument Valley as the primary location for his Westerns. The intrinsically noble geological features – Rooster Rock, Meridian Butte, Totem Pole, The Mittens, King on His Throne, Big Indian, Bear and the Rabbit – became a landscape given meaning through Ford's camera. No other location so immediately evokes the American West. Ford would return there even when he wasn't working on a film – Harry Goulding reserved a little stone building for him that was visible from the front door of the trading post and looked out over the Valley. In later years, one particular location, where Ford enjoyed setting up his camera, was given the name Ford's Point.

Ford shot *Stagecoach* from 31 October to 23 December 1938, 47 shooting days, four days over schedule, for a budget of slightly less than $550,000. Ford was paid $50,000 plus 20 percent of the profits, Dudley Nichols was paid $20,000 and the cast, in toto, received $80,000, only $3,700 of which was allocated to John Wayne, who was paid just about what he was getting at Republic.

Although Ford made Wayne's life miserable during the shooting, he also made his career possible. Anytime there was a chance for a reaction to a moment in the

On the set of 'Wee Willie Winkie' (1937)
During the filming of this Shirley Temple vehicle in the Santa Susanna Mountains (Temple is standing on camera track), an executive visited the set and said John Ford (seated to the right of the camera track) was behind schedule. "How many pages?" asked Ford. He was informed it was four pages of the script. Ford carefully counted out one, two, three, four pages, ripped them out and handed them to the man, and said, "We're on schedule. Now beat it." And he never did film those pages.

ABOVE
Still from 'The Hurricane' (1937)
The hurricane hits the island and the islanders try to survive by tying themselves to a tree. Huge propellers sent wind, water and sand at the actors with such force that sometimes little pinpricks of blood were left on their skin.

LEFT
On the set of 'The Hurricane' (1937)
Ford had a habit of sitting in front of the camera under the lens. Not only could he see what the camera was filming but when he yelled "Cut!" he habitually raised his fist in front of the lens. This effectively meant that the studio could only use the film between the slate at the beginning and Ford's fist. Since he only ever used one angle, it meant that the studio had to use exactly what he wanted them to use. Most of the film was shot on sets with a few Samoan background shots for authentication.

film, or a response to another character, Ford would insert a shot of Wayne, making him the focal point of the scene. Ford told Wayne that context was everything, that he didn't really have to express all that much – that the audience would read into him whatever emotion the scene indicated.

From the trade papers to newspapers all over the world, the film was hailed as an instant classic, especially the 8-minute, 48-second chase. Certainly, it made John Wayne a major star, and from the stunning entrance Ford gives the young actor – the camera rapidly dollying into a tight close-up as Wayne flourishes his rifle – that was the clear intention.

Ford and Nichols juggle a lot of characters and a fair amount of plot, but everything is written and played with delicacy and truth. Ford has less time for the photographic beauty that would come to dominate his work; the camerawork tends more toward functional storytelling than it does the pyrotechnics of overt composition, except for the rapid track-in to John Wayne: Ford's proudly emphatic announcement of a star being born. But nearly 70 years haven't changed the fact that *Stagecoach* is the paradigmatic Western. As André Bazin wrote of it, 'Art has found its perfect balance, its ideal form of expression.'

Ford would make deeper films than *Stagecoach,* and he would make more virtuosic movies than *Stagecoach*, but he would never again make one so nearly perfect, more filled with an easeful grace, with a perfectly inflected camera and characters. It is his *City Lights* (1931), his *Rules of the Game* (1939), but unlike those pictures, which don't fall into any neat genre classification, the characters and settings of *Stageocach* could be all too easily replicated by other, less expert hands, and in fact were, hundreds of times during the succeeding decades in movies or television. This accounts for the way that *Stagecoach* has of seeming something of a twice-told tale these days.

But *Stagecoach* gave Ford a subject that meshed perfectly with his calm style. Ford had been experimenting with two- and three-plane composition for some time, often holding sharp focus throughout. His collaborations with cameraman Gregg Toland on *The Long Voyage Home* and *The Grapes of Wrath* would extend the style still further. But *Stagecoach* was a completely integrated example of the style – one of the reasons Orson Welles looked so intensively at the film before embarking on *Citizen Kane* (1941).

It was a style particularly suited to Ford's aesthetic and emotional sensibilities: meditative compositions in depth, usually medium shots, with the characters reacting to each other within the shot. It gave the actors more to work with, and gave the studio less. From this point on, Ford's camera would be predominantly still, so that when he did move it – the sudden, quick pan to the Indians on the cliff, the furious tracking shots during the attack – the simple fact of the movement would add excitement to the scene.

Stagecoach fired the starting gun for the career of John Ford as a completely integrated artist. No more would he direct make-good projects – *The Whole Town's Talking, Submarine Patrol* – which could only be approached as "a job of work". He chose now to unleash a fully developed directorial personality; picturesque, ample, meditative, self-assured films of history and longing composed with what John Wayne would call Ford's "simplicity of delivery". His characters would go about their business with a mournful weight, befitting the grandeur of the stage on which they were playing.

Still from 'Four Men and a Prayer' (1938)
Four sons travel the world in an attempt to clear their father's name and avenge his murder. Here Christopher Leigh (David Niven, centre) and Lynn Cherrington (Loretta Young) watch Geoff Leigh (Richard Greene) shoot a man. It was "a job of work" for Ford.

For Ford, America and democracy grew out of the encounter between wilderness and civilization, and Monument Valley became the meeting ground for the palpable and the possible. The complexity of the pictures he was about to make meant that John Ford's themes were, at long last, the full equal of his images.

After *Stagecoach,* Ford went back to Fox for *Young Mr. Lincoln* (1939). Ford and Zanuck settled on a light makeup for Henry Fonda, mostly around the nose, that suggested Lincoln more than it replicated him. Lincoln's future derives from his past – from his memory of Ann Rutledge, the girl he left behind in the graveyard in New Salem. In Ford's work, the dead are palpable influences for the living, if only because their hopes and dreams must be carried forward.

Many writers have opted for a fairly simplistic reading of Ford, claiming that his work progressed from optimism to pessimism as he aged. But this overlooks how the optimism in his earlier works is almost always tempered with a sense of loss. In any case, Ford's celebrations of community and the community's future are always set in the past, never the present. The greater the optimism, the further in the past the story. Film-making, not alcohol, was Ford's primary narcotic, and nostalgia his primary emotion.

There is something that feels right about Ford's Lincoln; he imposes his will without seeming to, has a gift for the jugular as well as for leisure, and he is no backwoods saint – he takes money for defending his client even though the family is poor. This is a Lincoln who lives in the real world – even lawyers have to eat.

Ford and Henry Fonda continued their collaboration with *Drums Along the Mohawk* (1939), an adaptation of a best-selling historical novel and the director's first experience in Technicolor. The film is beautifully arranged, but Ford always remained somewhat distrustful of colour, calling black and white "real photography". The film is his sole excursion into the sadly under-utilized subject of the Revolutionary War, and if Claudette Colbert's innate stylishness feels too artificial for a Ford film, it's hard to criticize it otherwise. John Carradine's villain is nothing if not picturesque in a black cloak and eye patch, and Ford even steals a signature shot from King Vidor's *The Big Parade* (1925), as Colbert falls to her knees in supplication as her man goes off to war, just as Renee Adoree did with John Gilbert.

The extensive location work in Utah gives the film an airy, relaxed feel, meshing well with the vigorous action footage. *Drums Along the Mohawk* is a fine example of Ford the professional film-maker rather than the pure artist.

The studio system had its weak points, but one example of its benefits is how it could customize pictures for favoured talents – not just actors, but directors as well. Case in point: Ford completed *Drums Along the Mohawk* on 5 September 1939. He had precisely four weeks before the beginning of production on *The Grapes of Wrath* (1940). This meant that producer Darryl Zanuck essentially ramrodded pre-production, from the writing of Nunnally Johnson's script, to most of the casting, to the art direction of Richard Day.

John Steinbeck's novel had been published in 1939 and quickly became a sensation. Zanuck maintained an aura of secrecy around the project, ordering Nunnally Johnson to make only three copies of the script. It appears that Ford may not have been Zanuck's first choice as director; a notation on a studio copy of the script has a teasing notation: 'Clarence Brown?' referring to the premier MGM director, whose films such as *Ah, Wilderness* (1935) and *Of Human Hearts* (1938) had marked him as among the most lyrical Hollywood talents.

ABOVE
Still from 'Submarine Patrol' (1938)
A not-too-convincing model shot from a film that Ford once named as a favourite. Like 'Men Without Women' and 'Seas Beneath', it has an authentic feeling of male camaraderie in times of crisis.

PAGES 106/107
Still from 'Stagecoach' (1939)
The stagecoach is escorted by the US cavalry (led by Tim Holt) through Monument Valley. Although it makes a large impression in the film, only seven days of the 47-day shoot took place there. For Ford, this film was a variation of the Guy de Maupassant story 'Boule de suif', the story of a prostitute who sleeps with a Prussian officer so that she and her fellow passengers on a stagecoach can proceed safely. The passengers force her to sleep with the officer, and then loathe her afterwards, thus revealing their hypocrisy. In his film, Ford reveals the hypocrisy of society and the virtues of those outside society.

But after some initial hesitance, Ford accepted the job, largely because he could relate to the material. "The whole thing appealed to me – being about simple people – and the story was similar to the famine in Ireland, when they threw the people off the land and left them wandering on the roads to starve."

Production began 4 October 1939. Working efficiently, Ford and the great cameraman Gregg Toland (borrowed from the Samuel Goldwyn Studios) fell into a perfect working rhythm. Mornings were taken up with long and medium shots, to get the delicate slanting light. Midday was reserved for close-ups, and then late in the afternoon it was back to long and medium shots. Each shot was rehearsed three or four times, and there weren't more than a couple of takes per shot. There was no make-up on the actors, no diffusion on the camera. Toland was shooting the picture sharp, hard and cold, to match the still photographs that Dorothea Lange and other photographers had taken of the Okies.

Ford was unusually attentive to the nuances of his actors; at one point he directed Eddie Quillan, playing Rosasharn's hapless husband, to "Get your voice a little on the Southern." A run-through brought another direction: "Make it stronger."

Likewise, when Rosasharn's husband leaves her with a baby and not much else, Ford sat just outside of camera range and took the actress' hand. "Poor Rosasharn. She has so much to deal with. He's just left you. He walked out. It was too much for him. He couldn't face not being able to feed you, and having a baby. You're alone now, and although you've got Ma and Tom and Pa, Grandma's gone, but you know that you may not be able to feed your baby. You're lost, you're lost. You don't know this land. Ma may not be able to hold on. This is for the long shot. Now you read those lines to me." He was reverting to the technique of the silent era, talking the actor into and through an emotional moment.

Ford directed John Carradine as Casey to get down on his haunches and spread his arms like a spider. Carradine often resisted Ford's directions – the two men had a love-hate relationship based on their mutual stubbornness and shared Irish heritage, as well as the fact that Carradine had an ego nearly the equal of Ford's. The other actors thought Ford was pushing Carradine over the line into caricature, but the physicality of his role isn't silly, it's startlingly original and fascinating. Casey is a man in his own space, in his own world, living by his own rules, unconcerned about what others think. His sprawling, relaxed physicality is the yin to Tom Joad's tightly coiled yang.

As for Henry Fonda, Ford left him alone. The actor was a proud, stubborn, slightly chilly man who felt Tom Joad without prompting from his director. Fonda's Joad combines the Midwestern sincerity of his Lincoln with an ex-con's cold paranoia. He's no victim, is in fact perfectly capable of making a lot of trouble. Fonda's lean equalizer is the main reason the film never subsides into a morass of little-people sentimentality, the reason it still speaks with surprising immediacy.

For the all-important final scene between Tom Joad and his mother, Ford left it to the actors, refusing to watch them rehearse, holding off the shooting to make sure that the actors were on edge. "We'd never done it out loud," remembered Henry Fonda, "but Ford called for action, the cameras rolled, and he had it in a single take. After we finished the scene, Pappy didn't say a word. He just stood up and walked away. He got what he wanted. We all did."

Ford completed *The Grapes of Wrath* in 43 days of production, and it opened on 24 January 1940, barely five weeks later. The film was immediately hailed as a

ABOVE
Publicity still for 'Stagecoach' (1939)
When escaped convict Ringo (John Wayne) sees prostitute Dallas (Claire Trevor) with Mrs Mallory's newborn baby, he professes his love for her and asks to marry her. After the plot of the film is finished, these outsiders leave to start a family of their own. As Doctor Josiah Boone says, somewhat sarcastically, they have been "saved from the blessings of civilisation."

OPPOSITE TOP
Still from 'Stagecoach' (1939)
The film is best remembered for the exciting chase across a salt lake, with the Indians trying to kill the occupants of the stagecoach. Here Ringo is defending the people who want to put him back in jail.

OPPOSITE BOTTOM
Still from 'Stagecoach' (1939)
The stunts in the film were organised by Yakima Canutt. As well as jumping, at 45 miles per hour, from a horse to the lead horse of a team, and falling to the ground to let the stagecoach roll over him (as an Indian), and jumping from the coach forward to the front horses (as Ringo), he executed spectacular horse falls like this one.

masterpiece, although it was not a big financial success, grossing about twice what it cost – it was a little too rigorous, a little too uncompromising.

Nunnally Johnson's script subtly shifts the focus from Ma to Tom, to accommodate the fact that Ma is being played by a character actress while Tom is being played by a star. Ford emphasizes the dignity of the people that work the land, and their sense of loss when that work is taken away. The film lacks the sociological sting of the novel, but it compensates by creating a feel of universality, making the Joads archetypes of dispossession.

Ford's touch for metaphor was never as sure or as delicate. The people who come to throw the Okies off their lands remain encased in their cars or their caterpillar tractors, agents of the machine. Muley and his family stand on the ground they have struggled to farm, defenceless, without armour.

At the end of Steinbeck's book, Casey is dead, Tom has been beaten and Rosasharn's stillborn baby is floating down a river. At the end of Ford's movie, Tom leaves his family to organize a union, but Ford makes his gradual abstraction seem as real as the dirt that the desperate, blasted Muley sifts through his fingers. Tom is one of Ford's men on the border, doomed, like Ethan in *The Searchers* (1956), to live his life poised between wilderness and society. When Tom goes over the hill, he becomes another one of Ford's fierce ghosts in the American darkness.

In early 1940, Walter Wanger signed a contract with Argosy mandating that Ford would direct *The Long Voyage Home* (1940), an adaptation of several one-act plays by Eugene O'Neill.

By the time Argosy signed the contract with Wanger, Ford already had Dudley Nichols working on the screenplay, a rather smooth conversion of four one-act plays (*The Moon of the Caribees*, *Bound East for Cardiff*, *The Long Voyage Home* and *In the Zone*) into one script.

The Long Voyage Home is among the most relentlessly photographed movies in Ford's career; every shot is a knockout. Some critics, David Thomson among them, object to Ford's showing off, believing that the tail of the image is wagging the dog of the story. But given the cramped location of the film – most of the movie takes place on board a ship – visual variety is necessary if the viewer isn't to get bored.

Ford and Toland worked in complete harmony and in a completely different style than their previous collaboration. *The Grapes of Wrath* feels like a documentary, but *The Long Voyage Home* is close to the stylized, *echt*-UFA style Ford had utilized for *Hangman's House*. When the crew had to shift lights for another set-up, Ford and Toland would huddle, Toland looking through his viewfinder, then passing it over to Ford for his agreement. When the lights were ready, the actors would rehearse while Ford watched, rubbing his face as if it itched. Toland moved in and out of the group, taking readings with his light meter. Ford would finally say, "Let's try it." After a run-through, he'd make adjustments, giving the actors more pieces of business, occasionally demonstrating what he wanted them to do.

The latitude Ford gave Toland to work in his favourite deep-focus style disproves the myth of Ford as rigid authoritarian – he was usually much harder on actors than he was on his crew. Ford adored Toland; the cameraman had an innate eye for composition and, like Ford, he worked decisively. It was a case of one artist delighted to be working with another artist.

There is a considerable difference in texture on Ford's films, even in the same period, from the shadowed, soft look Joe August gave Ford on *The Informer*, to the

ABOVE
Still from 'Young Mr. Lincoln' (1939)
Abe Lincoln (Henry Fonda) talks to his lost love Ann Rutledge, who died before they could make a life together. She seemed to know him best, and pushed him forward to achieve his deepest ambitions. Lincoln balances a stick over her grave saying that if it falls towards her, he would become a lawyer. It does, and he concedes that maybe he helped it a little.

OPPOSITE
Publicity still for 'Young Mr. Lincoln' (1939)
Henry Fonda had reservations about playing such an iconic figure from American history but, as Ford plainly told him: "You think you'd be playing the goddamn great emancipator, huh? He's a goddamn fucking jack-legged lawyer in Springfield, for Christ's sake!"

LEFT
Still from 'Drums Along the Mohawk' (1939)
The people of the Mohawk valley seek refuge in a fort during the 1776–1781 War of Independence. On the right can be seen Gil Martin (Henry Fonda), Adam Hartmann (Ward Bond) and Joe Boleo (Francis Ford). Despite repeated setbacks (Indian attacks, fires burning crops and houses, marching off to battle and losing more than half the men, being besieged by English-led Indians) the people stoically remake their society so that they can live the life they want.

PAGES 114/115
Still from 'The Grapes of Wrath' (1940)
The eviction of Oklahoma tenant farmers, their migration to California and their fight for life, liberty and the pursuit of happiness is, in John Ford's hands, similar to the flight of the Irish from their homeland because of the great famine. In this scene Pa Joad (Russell Simpson), Tom Joad (Henry Fonda) and Uncle John (Frank Darien) are in a camp for transients, listening to a man being backed up by officers of the law as he offers them illegal exploitative wages.

diffused and glowing Bert Glennon pictures (*The Hurricane*, *Young Mr. Lincoln*) to Toland's high-contrast, razor-focused work in *The Long Voyage Home* and *The Grapes of Wrath*.

It is clear that there would have been no *Citizen Kane* without Toland's experiments on *The Long Voyage Home*. Although *Citizen Kane* is shot with a harder focus, the photographic style is virtually identical. During production on *Citizen Kane*, Toland was constantly taking a leaf from Ford's book and telling Welles to play a scene "in one" i.e. in one shot, without cutting, whenever possible and avoid unnecessary editing.

Ford and O'Neill were something of a dream pairing, sharing an essentially tragic view of life born out of an Irish Catholicism that is equal parts anger, guilt, repression and submission. The men on the *Glencairn* are largely either reformed or haunted alcoholics, united only in their resolve to make sure that a young Swede named Ole not be trapped as a sailor like they are. The rest of them are caught between their mutually exclusive desires for home and their yearning for the sea.

John Wayne's Ole is the pampered child of the other crewmen. Ole is protected from drunkenness, Ole is rescued when shanghaied. It may be too late for the others but, by God, Ole will survive and thrive – they will see to it. It is this protective dynamic that gives the film its through-line, gives the characters a feeling of self-sacrificing family within an otherwise sensual mood.

Ford captures the mutual dependence of men at sea, the bonds of trust and reciprocal discretion, the unspoken devotion, as well as the vulnerability that lies just beneath the skin. As Ward Bond's Yank lies dying, he doesn't want to be alone. It's a film of dark diagonals and even darker fate, a visual masterpiece and very close to a dramatic one as well.

Ford received Oscar nominations for both *The Long Voyage Home* and *The Grapes of Wrath*, but won for the latter. He didn't show up; he was fishing off the coast of Mexico with Henry Fonda.

After *Tobacco Road* (1941), the single abortive picture from this period, notable solely for some stunning photography oddly out of synch with the raucous, trashy comedy that is at the heart of the material, Ford moved on to *How Green Was My Valley* (1941), the culminating achievement of this period, and his last film before service in World War Two.

Both the script and much of the casting for *How Green Was My Valley* were done under the supervision of William Wyler, who was originally slated to direct. As screenwriter Philip Dunne said, "Wyler did everything except actually shoot it." But Zanuck was unhappy with Wyler's taste for elaboration in the script and strove to keep the focus on the people. Wyler left the picture shortly after the key casting of Roddy McDowall for the part of the child through whose eyes we see the picture. The money people in New York were nervous about the script, nervous about the plot involving union organizing, nervous about the lack of star names in the cast, and especially nervous about Wyler's reputation for extravagance in production time. They refused to spend the money. Zanuck was furious and informed the New York office that he would make the picture one way or the other, even if he had to make it at another studio.

There was only one director who could shoot the film for the money Zanuck could spend and not cut corners. Zanuck offered Ford $100,000 on a separate contract for this one film only, $15,000 more than he was currently paying Ford for a picture.

Publicity still for 'Tobacco Road' (1941)
Lov Bensey (Ward Bond) and Ellie May Lester (Gene Tierney) are lovers in this low comedy which was one of the low points in Ford's œuvre.

"Ford was a caricature more than a character. He deliberately dressed down and deliberately drove a Buick instead of a Cadillac, not wanting to give in to the Hollywood lifestyle."

Charles FitzSimons

At the end of August 1941, the last shot was completed, almost exactly eight weeks after the cameras had rolled. "It was the most succinct production experience I have ever encountered," remembered Roddy McDowall. Ford had taken precisely two months to shoot a picture that any other director would have shot in three, and Wyler would have shot in four, and with no sacrifice in visual or dramatic quality. The film was released in December to rapturous critical and commercial response.

Richard Day's production design gives *How Green Was My Valley* an epic sweep, and Ford's eye gives it a sense of reality. He gets a sense of both emotion and physical detail in it, does so many things right: the men tossing their pay into the mother's apron as she waits by the door of the house; the women of the town reaching out to touch the splendour of Bronwyn's wedding dress; the chirruping fear of Huw when he believes he won't walk again; the sluggish, stunned movements of the men after they've gone on strike – tradition breaking apart on the shoals of the twentieth century.

How Green Was My Valley is largely a story of dispersal and dissolution, but it's a tribute to Ford's powers of suggestion that he could convincingly create an aura of warmth and nostalgia around a movie about bad marriages, poverty, fatal mining accidents and violent, family-rending labour disputes, without ever actually betraying the tone of the material.

Ford could glide from the more or less scathing left-wing viewpoint of *The Grapes of Wrath* to the uneasy centrism of *How Green Was My Valley*, where the unions are justified but bring a heavy cost, because his vision was always more communal than collective, and almost never political. In that sense, his lionization by the left in the mid-1930s in the wake of *The Informer* was a misunderstanding that worked to Ford's critical advantage.

Criticisms that the film is an inaccurate depiction of a mining town are largely irrelevant; it is explicitly about life seen through the eyes of a child. The characters are drawn with the broad strokes of an awestruck boy, bathed in the golden glow of an adult's remembrance of his childhood. And the film also serves as one of the most cogent statements of Ford's deepest theme: the way that time's flow destroys the old ways, which must die in order for the future to take hold.

The run of films that began with *Stagecoach* completed Ford's transition from excellence to greatness. The back-to-back Academy awards for direction were an achievement that has not been equalled, and he now stood at the apex of the American film industry, in complete synch with his industry and his culture.

But World War Two would end all that; by the late 1940s there would be no general cultural consensus, no sense of social and aesthetic unity that could encompass political radicals as well as mainstream values. America's divisions became more pronounced, and John Ford's belief in America's lambent promise would darken.

ABOVE
Still from 'How Green Was My Valley' (1941)
Huw Morgan (Roddy McDowall) is ill after falling through the ice. He fills his time by living in books, much as John Ford had done as a child when he missed a year at school due to diphtheria.

PAGES 120/121
Still from 'How Green Was My Valley' (1941)
After Mr Gruffydd (Walter Pidgeon, right) carries Huw up a hill to see daffodils there is a magical moment when Huw begins walking again. The idyllic ambience owes much to Ford's use of the camera to present the foreboding story and events through the eyes of an optimistic young boy. In fact, Mr Gruffydd fails as Huw's moral centre and leads Huw into a life of self-denial and misplaced nostalgia.

Mister Ford
1942–1956

There was really no doubt about which branch of the service Ford would serve in. In June 1934, he had bought a 110-foot ketch called *Faith* that he rechristened the *Araner*. She quickly became his most valued possession. This man who habitually dressed in a manner verging on the slovenly spared no expense to make the *Araner* gleam. Her hull was painted white, and her superstructure was all varnished teak, with a central salon anchored by a large poker table. The ship carried a crew of six to take care of the in-line diesels that powered the ship. Ford refitted her at considerable expense, overhauling the engines, putting in a new mast, rebuilding the bow and stern, adding a deckhouse and having the bottom recoppered.

The *Araner* had two fireplaces, two bathrooms, red carpets, a four-poster bed, and a dressing room for Mary. Other directors spent their money on women or gambling, but the *Araner* would be Ford's designated luxury. It was a vacation hideaway, an alternate home, a refuge, a cabin in the woods. Here, Ford would while away a good part of the next 30 years, arranging his schedule so that he could spend several weeks or a month at a time on board the yacht, usually docked either in Catalina or Honolulu.

At the same time, Ford enlisted in the Naval Reserve. He got a commission as a lieutenant commander and dove into the life of a gentleman sailor with alacrity, buying every uniform the Navy offered, and assiduously currying favour with his superior officer. He bestowed an oil painting of the USS *Constitution* on the Officer's Mess of the Armory in Los Angeles; he bestowed theatre tickets and studio passes, even taking Captain Claude Mayo to Catalina on board the *Araner*.

The meaning behind all this was clear: the pomp and circumstance of the Navy would represent a deeper validation than the movies. While Ford was turning out a succession of great movies with a deceptive nonchalance, he was also keeping an eye on the storm coming from Europe. In December 1939, he wrote a report indicating that he had been doing some light reconnaissance for the Navy during a cruise to Baja on board the *Araner*.

At about the same time, Ford began organizing what he called the Field Photo Service and enlisted a group of men in the film industry, among them Gregg Toland, Robert Parrish and 200 other men. For a full year, the men in Ford's unit underwent training in whatever aspect of film work they didn't already know. The sessions were held on an old soundstage at Fox, or the Naval Reserve Armory in Los Angeles. At

On the set of 'The Long Gray Line' (1955)
John Ford (right) shows Ward Bond (behind him) how to hit Tyrone Power (left). Ford acted like a tough guy, and enjoyed the drinking, fighting and camaraderie. This was a front for him to hide his compassion and sensitivity. The slouched hat and dark glasses also helped him to conceal his true emotions from others.

"A genius between 'Action!' and 'Cut!' Other times, an interesting human being. Tortured – wild and crazy. But when he said 'Action' something magical happened."

Michael Wayne

ABOVE
Still from 'December 7th' (1943)
The attack on Pearl Harbour propelled America into World War Two. Only 450 feet of actual battle footage existed, but through dramatic reconstructions director Gregg Toland and writer/producer Samuel G. Engel turned this film into an 85-minute propaganda piece that criticised the Navy and was consequently shelved. Ford edited together a 34-minute cut for public consumption, but made sure that the long version was preserved for future generations.

RIGHT
On the set of 'This Is Korea!' (1951)
Although John Ford (left) wrote that he was going to film a 'narrative glorifying American fighting men' in Korea he typically added a note of defeat and asked the question, via the narration, "Well, what's it all about? You tell us."

the end of the year, each of the nine divisions was a complete camera unit, able to undertake all aspects of documenting a war with motion picture or still cameras, from 35mm Mitchells and Bell & Howells to 16mm Eyemos, Akeleys and DeVrys. They could develop and print their work in the field or on board ship. They were even indoctrinated in Navy routine, although Ford's grasp of that would always be casual, to say the least.

But the Navy was leery of a bunch of Hollywood amateurs, however well-meaning and well-trained. Finally, Colonel William Donovan, the legendary "Wild Bill", accepted Ford's unit as the photographic component of the Office of Strategic Services – the OSS, the precursor of the CIA. Ford's only superior was Donovan; Donovan's only superior was President Franklin D. Roosevelt.

On 9 September 1941, Donovan ordered that John Ford be put on active status and assigned to his office as soon as was convenient. Back in Hollywood, Zanuck wanted Ford to re-sign with Fox; RKO was after Ford alone or with Argosy; Jesse Lasky was after him on behalf of Warner Brothers to direct *The Adventures of Mark Twain*.

As a middle-aged man, Ford didn't have to enter the military and put his career on hold, but for him there were no second thoughts. Ford walked away from the work he loved and had always needed. Movies would have to wait. On 7 December 1941, Ford and his wife and daughter were having dinner at the home of Admiral Pickens in Alexandria, Virginia. The Admiral received a phone call telling him that Pearl Harbour had been attacked. Two weeks later, Ford was on his way to the Canal Zone. For the next three and a half years, John Ford's headquarters would not be 20th Century-Fox, or Argosy Productions, or Odin Street in Hollywood, but the OSS office at 25th and East streets in Washington D.C. and various and sundry points all over Europe and Asia.

Donovan was a man who valued creativity, intelligence and a love of adventure, and in return he gave his people a great deal of autonomy. Among his other recruits were the baseball catcher Moe Berg, Harvard president James B. Conant, and diplomats David Bruce and Allen Dulles. Once again, John Ford was in the right place at the right time. Over the next three years, Ford found himself at the Battle of Midway, in Algeria and North Africa and South America, and in India. Among other things, he supervised the photographic coverage of D-Day and 'flew the hump' to China.

The documentary films Ford made during the War were only occasionally boilerplate efforts, usually far more. Some of them are among his most interesting, deeply-felt films, and furthermore they are clearly John Ford films. *The Battle of Midway* (1942) offers the rough essence of Ford's spirit and the way he perceived the valour of the American mission. Ford shot much of the film himself, his 16mm Filmo loaded with Kodachrome. At one point, shooting from the island's powerhouse, a primary target of the Japanese bombers, he was hit in the head by a piece of flying concrete and knocked out. He recovered, picked up his camera and continued shooting, then was struck by shrapnel that ripped a three-inch hole in his upper arm. Ford made his way to the infirmary where he was treated and dosed with tetanus vaccine.

As a result of the circumstances under which it was made, *The Battle of Midway* does more than document the turning point of the war in the Pacific; it also has the necessary authenticity; as the explosions go off, the frame line of the 16mm film jumps within the camera mechanism. It has a very spare, aphoristic narration

"Ford adored a quality in himself: leadership. He wanted to be and was the admiral, on set and off, and he furthered that every split second, at anybody's expense."

Jack Lemmon

Still from 'The Battle of Midway' (1942)
Ford first screened the film for President Franklin D. Roosevelt and his wife Eleanor at the White House. At the last minute Ford spliced in a shot of their son, James Roosevelt, saluting the dead. Everybody was talking throughout this short film but when the Roosevelts saw their son, everybody went silent and the true nature of the film was revealed. The President said, "I want every mother in America to see this picture."

On the set of 'They Were Expendable' (1945)
Returning to Hollywood was difficult for Ford
(second left of camera), after commanding so
many men in a conflict that meant something.
He decided that all the money he earned making
this film should go to charity, and set up a home
for the men that Ford had commanded.

*"Ford was an enigma. You could never tell when
he would turn on you. But I liked him, and we all
respected him. If he wanted a startled expression
from you in a scene, he wouldn't tell you what he
wanted. He'd wait until you got into the scene
and then shoot a gun off right in back of you."*

Donald Curtis

compared to other, invariably hectoring wartime documentaries. Ford trusts the
image, trusts the mood conveyed by 'Red River Valley' played at sunset, trusts the
feelings associated with the voices of Henry Fonda, Jane Darwell and Donald Crisp.

The Battle of Midway earned superior notices, of which James Agee's is the most
apposite: 'The impact is quick as a wound and deep as loneliness,' he wrote in *The
Nation*. 'The result is a first-class failure to film the most difficult of all actions –
a battle. But it is a brave attempt to make a record – quick, jerky, vivid, fragmentary,
luminous – of a moment of desperate peril to the nation.' Along with John Huston's
The Battle of San Pietro, *The Battle of Midway* is one of the few World War Two
documentaries carrying the real reverberations of battle and death.

December 7th (1943) is a special case. The film was prepared and shot by Gregg
Toland as a 85-minute docudrama combining a history lesson about Hawaii with a
recreation of the attack on Pearl Harbour and a lot of accusations about the
supposed part Japanese-Americans had in the attack. The film was loathed by the
Navy brass, who felt that the film implied that the Navy had not been on the job.
Roosevelt issued a directive saying that all future Field Photo material had to be
subjected to censorship, lest it injure morale. As a reclamation project, Ford took the
picture over and cut it down to 34 minutes, concentrating on the scenes of salvage

and repair, completely losing the accusatory tone and reducing Toland's effort at a documentary epic to a footnote. (Ford realized that Toland's original version was not negligible and was responsible for its preservation.)

For D-Day, Ford assigned two of his men to be lead cameramen in the first wave of the Normandy landing – amazingly, neither was killed – planned and executed a parachute drop for a cameraman who went in behind enemy lines three days before the invasion to shoot the incoming troops, and fitted some of the landing craft with automatic cameras that would begin filming as soon as the ramps lowered.

"Photograph what you see," he told his men. "If you can see it, shoot it." During the actual invasion, Ford was on the battleship *Augusta*, then went ashore and moved inland with the American troops. The director George Stevens encountered Ford and was astonished at his bravado. Stevens remembered sheltering himself under a hedge in Normandy when he looked up and saw Ford standing full-height, calmly observing some fighting.

The war changed John Ford, as it did every one of his generation of directors who saw combat. In the personal sense, it was a crucible in which he had tested himself and earned better than a passing grade. It also began a shift in his emotional

Still from 'They Were Expendable' (1945)
Rusty Ryan (John Wayne, right) carries the dead body of Slug Mahan (Murray Alper) while under attack from the air. Ford chose to tell the true story of his friend Lieutenant John Bulkeley (Robert Montgomery as Lt. John Brickley), who commanded wooden PT boats in the Philippines and won the Medal of Honor for his actions. However, of the 111 men he commanded, only nine returned, and he felt bitter about this. Ford highlighted the theme of men sacrificing themselves for a lost cause. Indeed, the theme is in the film's title.

allegiance from that of a professional film-maker to the profession of arms, a conversion that would be amplified in June 1945, when he was promoted to the rank of Commander.

Most men wrap up their war experience and place it on a mental shelf, to be taken down at appropriate intervals. But Ford would always keep a full selection of Naval uniforms, beautifully tailored and impeccably maintained, which he wore at the drop of a VFW (Veterans of Foreign Wars) convention. He also manoeuvred to get medals, decorations and awards, expressing a naked desire for validation.

Ford also wanted a tangible tribute to the work his men had done. He bought eight acres of land in the San Fernando Valley and built the Field Photo Farm. It was an elaborate clubhouse complete with bar, swimming pool, tennis and badminton courts and baseball diamond, all surrounded by eucalyptus trees. The master bedroom was permanently reserved for Bill Donovan. In the den were thirteen glass cases, holding the medals awarded to each member of the Field Photo Unit who had been killed in the war. There was also a beautiful little chapel on the grounds.

The idealistic intent was to maintain ties between the men that had formed Ford's hearty band of brothers and broaden it out amongst their wives and children. Ford took an extremely active position in relation to the Farm and paid for improvements and upkeep out of his own pocket. The Field Photo Farm would be the site of festive July Fourths and Christmas celebrations, not to mention two beer blasts a month for years, until the men began dying off or wanted to spend their holidays with their families.

The war also enveloped him with a sense of larger purpose that was absent from a career in Hollywood. Once you had seen Omaha Beach and the concentration camps, compliantly going back to work for the Zanucks and Warners was impossible. It stiffened his resolve about the kind of director he wanted to be. The John Ford of the 1920s and 1930s had been happy directing three or four pictures for the studio for every one he had directed for himself. No more. From now on, the proportions would be reversed.

Within a year of war's end, John Huston would form Horizon Pictures with Sam Spiegel; Frank Capra, George Stevens and William Wyler would be allied in Liberty Productions; Hitchcock would form Transatlantic Productions; and Ford and Merian C. Cooper would reactivate Argosy Productions. Argosy had already been responsible for two artistically successful pictures – *Stagecoach*, an Argosy effort in everything but name, and *The Long Voyage Home*.

But some things never changed. When the war ended, John Ford was 51 years old, with the same values he had always had. "I try to make people forget they're in a theatre," Ford said. "I don't want them to be conscious of a camera or a screen. I want them to feel that what they're seeing is real."

Back home in Hollywood, Ford would attend church two or three Sundays a month, then drive out to the San Fernando Valley to visit his sisters. He made yearly trips back to Portland to see his brother Pat and other acquaintances. He never talked about the movies, but rather old times. He liked family, but was more favourably disposed toward family he didn't have to support.

When it came to sports, it was baseball all the way – he would become a season ticket holder for the Dodgers when they moved to Los Angeles in 1958. When it came to food, it was lobster, or meat and potatoes, and his preferred non-alcoholic drink was ginger ale. Like most alcoholics, when he wasn't drinking he had a tremendous sweet tooth, and loved chocolate and vanilla ice cream, with frequent Hershey bars.

ABOVE
Still from 'My Darling Clementine' (1946)
The barber (Ben Hall) shows Wyatt Earp (Henry Fonda) his new image. Earp was dirty and unkempt when he was a cowboy on the range with his brothers, but his physical transformation echoes the changes in Tombstone when schools and churches begin to replace brothels and saloons. It is the birth of civilisation.

OPPOSITE
Still from 'My Darling Clementine' (1946)
Henry Fonda was bored between set-ups, so he started balancing on the back two legs of his chair, switching his legs on the post. Ford saw this and decided to incorporate it into the scene. It is a "grace note", a poetic moment that serves no purpose of plot, but adds to character. After World War Two, Ford was confident enough to add many more grace notes to his films.

When not shooting a film, he tended toward the nocturnal and would read several books in an average all-night session. In fiction, he liked P. G. Wodehouse or Irish writers. Music tended to be for when he was drinking, and then it tended to be lachrymose Irish ballads. He spoke mediocre French, and Spanish with a Maine accent.

"His whole life was movies," his son Patrick would say ruefully and Ford admitted it was true. The only pride he ever allowed himself was over the quality of his images. "I still think I'm the best cameraman in the business," he said.

Because of his unresolved – and unresolvable – internal conflicts, Ford was a man in perpetual flight from his fragile inner life to his rock-solid professional life. Pain was to be concealed; malice was to be displayed. He had cronies and acquaintances, but few friends. Everybody who knew him knew that they didn't really know him.

Before Ford could give independence a try, he had two pictures to make for other people, a Navy movie for MGM, and one more picture for Darryl Zanuck on his old contract.

They Were Expendable (1945) is a quiet, impressionistic saga of the PT boats and their scrappy struggle in the Pacific, of Subic Bay and Corregidor and Bataan, a time early in the war when America was being battered. Ford believed in heroes, and he created a couple of believable ones in Brickley (Robert Montgomery, who actually served on PT boats during the war) and Rusty Ryan (John Wayne), his restless, irritable second-in-command. He does less well with his idolatrous portrait of General Douglas MacArthur, who is shown evacuating the Philippines backed by 'The Battle Hymn of the Republic', and accorded a reverence Ford hadn't offered to Lincoln. (Ford undercuts the worshipful mood somewhat when he has a star-struck sailor ask MacArthur to autograph his hat.)

The film is superbly shot by the great Joe August, with far gloomier lighting than the ubiquitous MGM high key. It reflects a grave formal beauty, and the images of battle capture the phosphorescence of the water in the far Pacific, in spite of the fact they were shot off Key Biscayne, Florida. And in the largely unspoken romance between Rusty and Donna Reed's nurse Sandy Davis, Ford captures a quality of muted longing that beautifully suggests the impossibility of sustaining any kind of relationship during a war.

Men die, John Wayne intones Robert Louis Stevenson's 'Home is the Sailor', Bataan surrenders and the Japanese move on to Corregidor. Brickley and Ryan are airlifted out, leaving their men behind. "The job," Brickley says by way of farewell, "is to get ready to come back." Thus ends one of Ford's most stirring tributes to a lost campaign.

The most famous 30 seconds of the Old West took place in Tombstone, Arizona in October 1881.

The gunfight at the OK Corral involved the Earps and the Clantons. The Earps were attempting to arrest the Clanton faction, who had been walking around town for two days armed and dangerous, in clear violation of an ordinance outlawing guns within the city limits. When the smoke cleared, everybody but deputy sheriff Wyatt Earp was dead or wounded. A few weeks later, Virgil Earp was shot again, and Morgan Earp was killed. Virtually every dramatized version of the story would reverse the events, and have the OK Corral as the climax of the conflict rather than the opening salvo.

"I like to have the shadows black and the sunlight white. And I like to put some shadows into the light."

John Ford

OPPOSITE TOP
Still from 'The Fugitive' (1947)
In a country where religion is outlawed, a priest (Henry Fonda) is constantly on the run while trying to practice his faith. He is helped by a woman (Dolores Del Rio), who used to be the mistress of the soldier who hunts him. She is a personification of the Madonna/whore iconography that is found in many works by Irish Catholics.

OPPOSITE BOTTOM
Still from 'The Fugitive' (1947)
The whole film is bathed in an incandescent light courtesy of Gabriel Figueroa, Mexico's greatest cinematographer, who had studied under Gregg Toland and would later work with Luis Buñuel on seven films.

PAGES 132/133
On the set of 'Fort Apache' (1948)
Henry Fonda (left of camera with back to us) plays a headstrong cavalry colonel who disregards the warnings of more experienced officers in an effort to win glory for himself. Ford heavily researched the life and routine of a cavalry outpost and had his writers do detailed biographies for every character, no matter how small. This meant that the interactions of the characters gained the weight of history. In this rare colour photo, Fonda consults with John Ford (looking at us) whilst filming in Monument Valley.

ABOVE
Still from '3 Godfathers' (1948)
Robert Marmaduke Sangster Hightower (John Wayne, right) shows compassion for his dead friend William Kearney aka "The Abilene Kid" (Harry Carey, Jr., centre) by holding out his hat so that, in death, the kid can get some respite from the sun. They, along with fellow bandit Pedro Roca Fuerte (Pedro Armendariz), give up their chance to escape to save the life of a newborn baby.

RIGHT
Still from '3 Godfathers' (1948)
Hightower struggles on alone with the baby in this remake of the Harry Carey Western 'Marked Men'. Ford dedicated the film to his late friend Harry Carey and inducted Harry Carey, Jr. into the John Ford Stock Company.

My Darling Clementine (1946) is a remake of a 1939 Fox film called *Frontier Marshall*, with Randolph Scott as Wyatt Earp and Cesar Romero as Doc Halliday (the film's spelling). Efficiently but anonymously directed by Allan Dwan, it is a movie of limited interest, departing from history in a manner that makes the artistic impulses behind *My Darling Clementine* seem rigorously documentarian by contrast. Yet several sequences of Ford's film derive directly from Dwan's film, in particular the entire opening, with a drunken Indian terrorizing the town – Ford even hired the same actor, Charles Stevens, an old compatriot of Douglas Fairbanks – and the use of a visiting vaudevillian as a bone of contention between the two warring camps of Tombstone, Arizona.

Ford always denied seeing the original film, but he either saw it or read the script and kept ideas he knew could be strengthened.

Earp is one of the last times Ford would draw a man of the West without a character conflict; Earp has no particular nostalgia for the past and, except for the scene at his brother's grave – which wasn't directed by Ford – he never expresses any interest in the future. The Wyatt Earp created by Henry Fonda and John Ford is a self-possessed, pragmatic man, interested in a clean shave and a quiet town. If nobody else will give him those things, he'll have to provide them himself.

All the conflicts are embodied in the nearly urbane Doc Holliday, who inspires Earp with his education and covert graciousness even as he spirals down to self-destruction. To a great extent, Ford cast history aside and used only the premise of the gunfight at the OK Corral, for he knew that audiences – not to mention irascible film directors – want meaning more than facts. (*My Darling Clementine* is fanciful even by the limited standards of Hollywood. In real life, Old Man Clanton died several weeks before the gunfight, there was no Clementine and Doc Holliday didn't die in the gunfight.)

The Tombstone set constructed in Monument Valley cost $250,000. Ford's desire to help the Navajo played a considerable part in determining the location. It was the first film he'd made there since *Stagecoach*, and this time he was greeted on the steps of Goulding's as a friend.

Ford's sense of the texture of a scene, of the qualities a gifted actor can provide if you stand back and watch, was never sharper: Fonda leaning back in his chair on the sidewalk, balancing himself on a beam; the lengthy tracking shot of Earp and Clementine walking toward the half-built church, Fonda moving with the deliberate stride of a graceful stork.

Ford paces the entire picture to Fonda's purposeful, elegant rhythm. *My Darling Clementine* is a Westerner's Western – laconic, unfussy, large-spirited, and perennially modern in its quiet, contemplative mood and dark undercurrents. Nearly every exterior shot is framed to include vast expanses of sky, and in a particular masterstroke, the climactic gunfight is played without blaring music, but with only natural sounds – wind; boots scuffling for purchase in the sand. The silence is haunting.

From the El Greco skies of the opening scene, to the eminently jaunty, eminently soused tragedian Granville Thorndyke – the indispensable Alan Mowbray, who would encore the part in Ford's *Wagon Master* – to the resolutely underplayed ending, Ford keeps the focus on the people. Ford's direction is like the look on Fonda's face as Victor Mature (as Doc Holliday) finishes a Shakespearean soliloquy – attentive, observant, somehow beyond analysis. The meditative pace makes the spasms of savagery and violence, unusual for Ford's work, feel genuinely brutal.

"John Ford understood the idea of the beauty and the beast. He tried to convey the harshness of the land as well as the beauty. In Monument Valley he avoided the temptation to shoot nothing but breathtaking scenery. He had only an occasional beauty shot. They were like diamonds, valuable because they are rare."

Winton C. Hoch

Most of Ford's coaching seems to have gone into Victor Mature, who was Zanuck's preference for the part of Holliday, after Ford attempted to convince the producer that either Douglas Fairbanks, Jr. or Vincent Price would make a good tubercular gambler. Mature responds with his best performance, although he's about as tubercular as a Kodiak bear. His is a Doc Holliday on fire with a bad temper, furious with self-loathing over his illness and alcoholism. (It should also be said that Holliday is a great part that has given some journeyman actors – the aforementioned Cesar Romero, and more recently, Dennis Quaid and Val Kilmer – shining moments.)

My Darling Clementine gives human dimension to the myth of Wyatt Earp. *Stagecoach*, Lindsay Anderson observed, is very good prose, but *My Darling Clementine* is poetry. To extend the metaphor, *Stagecoach* was an overture, but *My Darling Clementine* marks the beginning of a ten-year period in which Ford would compose his definitive symphony of the legend of the American West.

Argosy's first post-war effort was *The Fugitive* (1947), an adaptation of Graham Greene's *The Power and the Glory*, a great novel of a tormented whiskey priest that could never have been filmed under the Production Code of that period (the priest fathers a child). Ford was undoubtedly thinking of a Catholic story of redemption à la *The Informer*, but with a bigger budget. However, in searching for a shootable equivalent to Greene's story, the best Ford and screenwriter Dudley Nichols could come up with was a priest whose only sin was an inability to believe in the coming of evil, in the form of a dictatorship. Acts of commission – alcoholism, whoring – were changed to a single sin of omission – silence – which made it impossible for the priest to command the fascination of the audience in the way that Gypo Nolan had.

Ford attempted to compensate by imposing an operatic style of photography on the picture. Sometimes stark, lusciously lit, always carefully composed on locations throughout Mexico, the film is a stillborn curio, dissolving from one over-the-top religious tableau to another, abandoning the actors amidst a profusion of picturesque silhouettes and shafts of light.

Americans tend to think of religion as something that is chosen, but Ford's religion was more in the European tradition – as part of the rhythm of his life, it chose him, which was one aspect of his problem in coming to grips with Greene's book. *The Fugitive* was a critical and commercial failure, forcing Ford to come up with more commercial material if Argosy Productions was to survive. The impetus forced him into some of his most profound contemplations of men and war.

Ford believed in the intrinsic worth of the military life; the war had stimulated his already strong sense of the community of men, and added a sense of the implicit air of potential tragedy hanging over every moment of a soldier's life. However, Ford's cavalry films are remarkably benign in their attitude to waging war: Colonel Thursday in *Fort Apache* (1948) is an arrogant, bitter man who gets himself and a lot of other men needlessly slaughtered; the entire plot of *She Wore a Yellow Ribbon* (1949) turns on avoiding a battle and bloodshed; *Rio Grande* (1950) involves military action, but only in response to continued attacks.

Fort Apache's exteriors were shot with a new infrared film, so that the sky photographed darker than it really was and the clouds looked like explosions in the sky. It made production more difficult – focus was tougher to hold, and make-up had to be specially made – but Ford was always willing to take pains with photography.

Fort Apache is a gloss on the Custer myth, with Lieutenant Colonel Owen Thursday portrayed as a churlish, brooding injustice collector – and not much of a soldier. By comparison, John Wayne's Kirby York is a good-humoured man, with body language that is far more relaxed. The film painstakingly recreates a sense of life on a distant cavalry outpost, and the rituals that maintain a sense of meaning and order in an otherwise godforsaken wilderness: points of military courtesy; dress uniforms worn for a post dance; morale-boosting songs while marching.

The film turns on the difference between Thursday and York: the latter believes Cochise to be an honourable man and makes promises; the former can't imagine the term being applied to an Indian, any Indian, and violates the promise, leading most of the company to destruction.

Thursday is doomed because he arrogantly attempts to impose his version of reality on an intransigent natural world far removed from his Eastern verities. Ford heroes played by Wayne – the Ringo Kid, Tom Doniphon, Nathan Brittles, even the ferocious Ethan Edwards – are never so vain as to attempt to bend the world to their will, preferring either an easy, mutual understanding or a proud exile – a function of Wayne's expansive spirit and humour.

But Henry Fonda's stiff walk sets him against the flow of life around him. In *Young Mr. Lincoln*, *The Grapes of Wrath* or *My Darling Clementine*, this translates to integrity; in *Fort Apache*, it translates to the tragic inhumanity of a martinet.

At the end, a reporter gazes at a portrait of Colonel Thursday, and calls him a great man and a great soldier. Kirby York pauses, and reflects on the truth. "No man died more gallantly," he says, confirming the legend, even though the legend is a lie.

Ford is a realist as well as a romantic poet. *Fort Apache* doesn't question the right of command; it simply acknowledges the complexities of command. Ford says that the lies are necessary, because the most important thing is that the greatest good happens for the greatest number of people. What's truly important is the flow of history, a new world being built on what has come before – sacrifices made, loves lost and families broken. People need myth as much as they need truth, maybe more. Unlike the famous epigraph of *The Man Who Shot Liberty Valance*, Ford prints both legend and fact, because that's where the peculiar strength of America lies – between idealism and pragmatism, between self-sacrifice and self-interest.

Fort Apache was a success, and instigated a change in Ford's *modus operandi*. He would increasingly rely on Westerns as a means of ensuring a healthy career, as well as a sort of extension of life on board the *Araner* – a life away from Hollywood, in the fresh air, with stuntmen and cowboys and other men of action that Ford admired.

Ford followed up *Fort Apache* with *3 Godfathers* (1948), a charming, quasi-religious reverie as well as a heartfelt fable of found family with a moving dedication that comes after the main title: 'To the memory of Harry Carey, Bright Star of the early western sky.'

Then came *She Wore a Yellow Ribbon* (1949), one of the director's most extraordinary visual achievements, although the script is really a loose collection of incidents. But Ford's grasp of his technique was so comprehensive that he shot a very physically complicated movie like *She Wore a Yellow Ribbon* in a month, averaging five to six script pages a day. The average for a large-scale studio picture was two to three pages per day.

She Wore a Yellow Ribbon is a reverse take on *Fort Apache*. The earlier film is about military disaster transmuted into heroism by posterity; *Yellow Ribbon* is about

ABOVE
**Still from 'When Willie Comes Marching Home'
(1950)**
In this comedy, Bill Kluggs (Dan Dailey) wants to
be a war hero but ends up as a gunnery
instructor.

LEFT
**Still from 'When Willie Comes Marching Home'
(1950)**
Over a weekend, Kluggs goes on a secret
mission, accidently parachutes into occupied
France, meets the Maquis Resistance in the
beautiful form of Yvonne (Corinne Calvet),
smuggles out top-secret microfilm of the V-2
rocket, and is back home within four days.

On the set of 'Wagon Master' (1950)
Upon its release few people saw 'Wagon Master' but it is one of Ford's most lyrical films, almost a series of "grace notes" lined up nose to tail. This rare colour shot shows Ford in his typical position just below the camera lens, directing the procession of wagons in the background.

a military success in which bloodshed is averted, but it's overweighed with a melancholy air of reverie and grief. The earlier film is about men in their prime, while the later film is about old men getting ready to retire. It is among Ford's most painterly movies, his way of compensating for the film's extremely loose, ballad-like structure – it's really nothing more than an accumulation of vignettes, some of surpassing loveliness.

After a time-passer back at Fox called *When Willie Comes Marching Home* (1950), Argosy embarked on *Wagon Master* (1950), one of the most relaxed and enjoyable of Ford's Westerns, an amiable folk tale about a wagon train of Mormons and the non-Mormons leading them: Ward Bond, Harry Carey, Jr. and Ben Johnson. It is a largely warm-hearted, easeful picture that gets its backbone from some unusually intense spasms of violence in its last third.

It's a lyrical ballad, an affirmation of Ford's essentially communal folk vision of America, where a dance or a graveside ceremony speaks more for the pioneers than all the dramatic battles in the world. (The motivation of most Ford heroes is social, not personal; journeys and wanderings, not vengeful quests for retribution – group odysseys.) Ford's Westerns are more about the West itself than they are about Western heroes. Ford's is a West you can believe in, a West of splintered floors and ragged, resolute people. Westerns were really Ford's vision of an idealized America – a democratic community of equals unified by a shared purpose.

Wagon Master is also an example of Ford's unusually clear-eyed view of relationships. In Ford's films, actual families – the Joads, the Morgans in *How Green Was My Valley*, the Weads in *The Wings of Eagles* – are usually destroyed by time and events. But found families, the families we choose for ourselves – *They Were Expendable*, *Wagon Master*, *The Quiet Man* – survive.

At the beginning of 1950, Argosy Productions signed a three-picture deal with lowly Republic Pictures, long the home of Gene Autry and Roy Rogers, mostly because it was the only way that Ford could get *The Quiet Man* made. Any studio would be happy to finance a John Ford Western, but John Ford in Ireland? The studios saw only another *Plough and the Stars* or worse, *The Fugitive*.

To prove his good will, Ford's first picture for Republic was another cavalry picture with John Wayne, a continuation of the character he played in *Fort Apache*. The script for *Rio Grande* seems a veiled metaphor for the Korean conflict. (Ford subsequently directed the on-the-spot documentary *This Is Korea!* (1951) and *Korea: Battleground for Liberty* (1959), an orientation film for soldiers stationed in Korea.) Just as many believed that Douglas MacArthur should have been allowed to use any means necessary to wipe out the North Korean Communists, so the character of Phil Sheridan is justified in saying, "I want you to cross the Rio Grande, hit the Apache and burn them out; I'm tired of hit and run, I'm sick of diplomatic hide and seek."

On the set of 'Wagon Master' (1950)
Elder Wiggs (Ward Bond, right) is the Mormon leader who is helped by Sandy Owens (Harry Carey, Jr., left) and Travis Blue (Ben Johnson) to shepherd a wagon train west to the promised land. The Mormons are forced west because of the racial prejudice and intolerance they encounter, and over the course of their journey they are joined by other outcasts. This theme of tolerance is in direct contrast to Ward Bond's real-life anti-Communist activities in the Motion Picture Alliance for the Preservation of American Ideals. John Wayne was a four-time president of the MPA and John Ford was an Associate Member, although he maintains he was there as a modifying influence.

Ford shot the film in a rapid 32 days in Moab, but the police action subtext is less important than the relationship between Kirby York and his estranged wife, a particularly mature portrait of a married couple who love each other but can't live together, an unspoken passion and devotion between two people that springs to life as they listen to a serenade of 'I'll Take You Home Again, Kathleen'.

Rio Grande was the beginning of a remarkable period of maturity in Ford's portrayals of women; the three films in which John Wayne was paired with Maureen O'Hara (*Rio Grande, The Quiet Man, The Wings of Eagles*) are all complex, mature explorations of all phases of adult love, from the strong sexual yearnings of courtship to the uneasy compromises of daily life to the bitter reality of separation and estrangement.

With another success, it was on to *The Quiet Man* (1952). Ford had played with the script for years. Maureen O'Hara remembered weekends on the *Araner* just after World War Two in which Ford would send the assembled children ashore, then put on some Irish records and dictate notes to O'Hara, who would type them up later. Ford hired Richard Llewellyn, the author of *How Green Was My Valley*, to write a first-draft script, then Frank Nugent to do the final draft.

Headquartered at Ashford Castle in County Mayo, much of the locations were in and around the village of Cong. As always, Ford insisted that everybody in the cast be in wardrobe and on the set every day, whether they were scheduled to work or not. Ford worked carefully on this picture, coping with the uncertain, drizzly nature of the light in Ireland. As assistant cameraman Ernest Day would remember, "If the weather was bad, we waited… when the weather cleared, off we went."

Ford knew the script backwards and forwards, but he also characteristically gave it room to breathe with carefully chosen bits of business dreamed up on the set, or taking advantage of a moment, as with the shot of John Wayne striding across the countryside to get his wife back. Spotting a beautiful green meadow with a pack of seagulls, Ford ordered the camera to be quickly set up and ordered Wayne to walk by the seagulls. All of them went up in the air simultaneously, offering a quick visual accent of beauty.

The company spent six weeks in Ireland, and John Wayne brought his four children over to the location to spend their summer vacations with their Uncle Jack.

A few weeks of work back at the Republic studios in Hollywood, and Ford had completed one of his most beloved films. *The Quiet Man* has never had to be rediscovered; each succeeding generation has accepted the film for the benevolent masterpiece it is, the audience finding the same joy as the film's hero, enmeshed in Ireland's warm green and desire's flaming red. It's a celebratory, festive film, literally expansive – the entire community shares in Sean Thornton's problems, and his joy in reconciliation with his wife.

Innisfree might as well be called Brigadoon, for it is a place apart from the world's cares. There is little on screen linking the place to the 20th century. Over the years, feminists, misled by the various boorish imitations of the film that were mounted by John Wayne – and once by Ford – have falsely accused *The Quiet Man* of being misogynistic – this for a film in which the main female character refuses to acquiesce to the prevailing order, or to her husband, until she gets what is rightfully hers.

The film is wise about the shifting nature of power in a sexual relationship, which makes it something more than a fairy tale – it is a fable of two people who cannot live together until they each learn humility and how to submit to each other. It's also

ABOVE
Still from 'Rio Grande' (1950)
The love story at the centre of the film is between Lieutenant Colonel Kirby York (John Wayne) and his estranged wife Kathleen (Maureen O'Hara). She is reunited with her husband after 15 years because she is chasing their son Jeff, who has enlisted in the army. They split because during the American Civil War Kirby followed orders and burned down her ancestral plantation. Kathleen cannot accept Kirby's sacrifice of self (and by extension his family) for duty to the regiment, but in the end she stands dutifully with the other women waiting for their men to come home.

OPPOSITE
Publicity still for 'Rio Grande' (1950)
When Indians kidnap children of the regiment, Kirby goes across the Rio Grande to rescue them. This action has since been interpreted as a comment on how Americans should wage war in Korea. (Note: The events in the publicity photo do not appear in the final film.)

ABOVE
Stills from 'The Quiet Man' (1952)
Sean Thornton (John Wayne) and Mary Kate
Danaher (Maureen O'Hara) begin their official
courtship under the watchful eye of matchmaker
Michaeleen Og Flynn (Barry Fitzgerald). Sean
and Mary Kate begin an argument and as Mary
is about to hit Sean, Michaeleen says to her,
"Have the good manners not to hit him until he is
your husband, and can hit you back."

LEFT
On the set of 'The Quiet Man' (1952)
Filming the opening sequence at Castletown
station. Several Ford films begin with a train
pulling into a station, including 'Doctor Bull' and
'The Man Who Shot Liberty Valance'.

an exile's dream of a land and people he had never known. It won Ford his last Oscar for Best Direction and became his greatest popular and critical success.

There was bound to be a slight anticlimax after *The Quiet Man*, and there was. Ford directed a remake of *What Price Glory* (1952) for Darryl Zanuck, but was unable to make a serious anti-war picture, as Raoul Walsh's 1926 original had been. Ford could have fun with soldiers, but not with war itself. Also, a certain air of unreality is created because Ford shoots the battles scenes on studio sets, and the comedy is too broad.

That air of unreality was maintained with Ford's remake of *Judge Priest*, entitled *The Sun Shines Bright* (1953), another one of his memory plays, although it's actually less a remake than a revision. The story takes place in Kentucky in 1896, but Ford gives the story the flavour of a generalized time remembered. The film is full of very late-in-the day racial stereotypes; Ford portrays the black people, along with the prostitutes, as the town's outcasts, yet he and Billy Priest clearly value the blacks as much as any of the other characters.

Narratively, it rambles, but Ford tones up the script with his visual grace. It is Ford uncut, the director at both his best and worst, making a film of memory and loss with characters haunted by their shared past – a poetic, deeply ordered vision where people are content with their place in society, where justice is fair and there's always room for genial eccentricity.

The film's centrepiece is a sequence of a whore's funeral that Ford had been trying to fit into a picture for years. Since we don't really know this prodigal daughter who has come home to die, the sequence has more of a poetic punch than an emotional one. Billy Priest believes that everybody, no matter how fallen, deserves an honourable send-off, and follows the hearse so that she can have the funeral she wanted. At first, he is the sole mourner, but one respectable citizen after another falls in behind the hearse, even the proper matrons. The scene is played naturalistically, the camera tracking quietly beside the growing phalanx of mourners, the only sounds footsteps, the tread of the horse pulling the hearse, the wagon wheels crunching stones and dirt. When they reach the church, Billy Priest delivers a eulogy that preaches forgiveness. It's probable that Ford made the entire movie for this single sequence, one of his greatest.

Mogambo (1953) was a great commercial hit, stoked by the potent combination of Clark Gable, Grace Kelly and Ava Gardner, but it has only trace elements of Ford. *The Long Gray Line* (1955) was the story of a minor functionary in the West Point athletic department for 50 years, an unpalatable cross between *It's a Wonderful Life* (1946) and *Goodbye, Mr Chips* (1939). It's notable as Ford's first film in CinemaScope, which he disliked. "You've never seen a painter use that kind of composition," he grumbled, comparing it to a huge tennis court.

Mister Roberts (1955) was far more promising, a great stage hit for Henry Fonda about the Navy in World War Two. Clearly, it was a dream pairing of subject and director. But Fonda wanted a more literal transcription of the play, and Ford wanted to make it larger, broader, and the disagreements ended with a fistfight between the two men on location on Midway Island.

Ford began drinking – one of the few times he didn't maintain sobriety while working – and just after the film returned from location, entered the hospital for gall-bladder surgery. The film was completed by Mervyn LeRoy, with retakes courtesy of Joshua Logan. Only the film's location footage was directed by Ford. Although the film was a financial success, it was a debacle for Ford and has come to

ABOVE
Still from 'The Quiet Man' (1952)
When Sean is knocked out by Red Will Danaher, an expressionistic flashback sequence explains why Sean does not want to fight – he killed a man in the boxing ring.

OPPOSITE TOP
Still from 'The Quiet Man' (1952)
Sean said "Good Morning" to Mary Kate, but her brother Red Will (Victor McLaglen) said Sean had "good night on his mind." A macho display of strength is a prelude to the big fight to come.

OPPOSITE BOTTOM
Still from 'The Quiet Man' (1952)
Mary Kate and Sean want to be free of the past. She wants her dowry and he needs to eradicate the fear he has of killing again. Both are resolved when Sean drags Mary Kate to her brother Red Will, gets the dowry and then participates in a Homeric fight. Here a woman offers Sean a "good stick to beat the lovely lady."

Still from 'What Price Glory' (1952)
John Ford had directed some second unit footage for Raoul Walsh's original 1926 silent film as well as for the 1932 sequel 'Hot Pepper'. He had also set up a tour of the play in 1949 for charity. Even though Ford was well versed in this World War One comedy drama, the tone of the piece felt wrong. The anti-war message was dissipated, although there are some resonant images (as in this photo of the graves of French soldiers). The sickly romance and the constant arguing of the central characters, played by James Cagney and Dan Dailey, seemed pointless.

be regarded as a missed opportunity. More importantly, the breach between Ford and Henry Fonda was permanent; they never worked together again.

As a result, in the latter stages of his career, Ford worked far more with John Wayne, which affected the kind of movies he made, as well as their reception. Fonda was a liberal as well as a respected actor who frequently returned to the stage. Wayne was regarded as a great star, a skilled screen presence, but not really an actor, and a political reactionary into the bargain.

Culturally snobbish critics assumed that Ford shared Wayne's politics, which wasn't necessarily the case, but as the 1950s gave way to the 1960s that assumption, and Ford's reliance on Westerns, which gradually came to be seen as a retrograde genre, meant both men would come to be regarded as cultural dinosaurs, out of step with the times.

In 1956, *The Searchers* was regarded as a good John Ford Western, nothing more. The popular taste ran toward spectaculars such as *Around the World in 80 Days* (1956) or Cecil B. DeMille's *The Ten Commandments* (1956). *The Searchers* was seen as a bread-and-butter picture executed with all of the director's usual craft, with, it is true, a better script than usual. In the nearly half century since, *The Searchers* has come to be regarded as among the primary movies of the post-war era, along with Hitchcock's *Vertigo* (1958) – another movie regarded at the time as the director's usual mixture. Movies both good (Ron Howard's *The Missing* (2003)) and bad (Paul Schrader's *Hardcore* (1979)) have used it as a foundation for their own structures.

Previous generations had responded to the great humanist statements of *The Grapes of Wrath*, the empathy of *Young Mr. Lincoln* and the easy, rollicking humanity of *The Quiet Man*. But later generations looked at those pictures and saw

Still from 'The Sun Shines Bright' (1953)
Lucy's mother (Dorothy Jordan) is a prostitute who comes home to die amid the intolerant townsfolk. In the most moving sequence of the film, Judge Priest leads her empty funeral procession but as he proceeds, one by one the community falls into step behind him.

Still from 'Mogambo' (1953)
Victor Marswell (Clark Gable) caresses Eloise Y. Kelly (Ava Gardner) in this tale of adventure and romance in Africa. The film grossed $5.2 million, more than any other John Ford film.

the venerated textbook classics of their fathers. They had to find their own Ford classics and did: *She Wore a Yellow Ribbon*, *The Man Who Shot Liberty Valance* and, supremely, *The Searchers* – a harsher film for harsher times.

In broad outline, *The Searchers* is a darkened, inverted version of *3 Godfathers* – both stories involve lengthy journeys through a hostile no-man's-land, with a child's rescue as motivation. But *3 Godfathers* is a sunny, consoling work with little violence, while *The Searchers* is a savage, disturbing film that projects all manner of psychological and physical hostility. The earlier film is well-executed melodrama motivated by selflessness; the latter is epic tragedy motivated by rage.

The primary differences between the novel and the film are the protagonist and the tone. Novelist Alan LeMay's hero is Martin Pawley, Ford's is Ethan Edwards, and the film version of the character is far darker than the novel's Amos Edwards, who in fact makes the idealistic speech about bringing civilization to the frontier that the movie gives to Olive Carey's Mrs Jorgenson. Primarily, Ethan wants to take revenge for the killing of his brother's family. Secondarily, he wants to kill his niece for becoming the squaw of the Indian chief Scar. This is entirely the invention of Ford and his long-time screenwriter – and former film critic with *The New York*

Times – Frank Nugent. Also deriving from the film-makers is Martin Pawley's Indian blood, and the sexual relationship between Debbie and Scar – in the novel she's his adopted daughter. Because of these changes, as well as making his lead character older and far more conflicted, in order to accommodate the presence of John Wayne, Ford shifts *The Searchers* from a simple story that verged on just-another-Western, to a far more complex exploration of racial and sexual tensions.

Ford knew *The Searchers* was something special. "We are busy working on the script of *The Searchers*," he wrote his friend Michael Killanin in March of 1955. "It's a tough, arduous job as I want it to be good. I've been longing to do a Western for quite some time."

Ford began production in Monument Valley on 13 June 1955 with 11 set-ups. From the beginning, the mood on the set was very serious, the tone intense. Wayne was playing something beyond any part he had ever attempted, but he had no trouble with the unforgiving obsidian at the core of Ethan Edwards. The character's righteous steel penetrated Wayne; although he had no interest in or much patience with Method acting, his responses during the production were very Method indeed. "He was even Ethan at dinner time," remembered Harry Carey, Jr. "He didn't kid around on *The Searchers* like he had done on other shows. Ethan was always in his eyes."

After his uncharacteristically unprofessional behaviour on *Mister Roberts*, Ford was at his rigorous best, working with the decisiveness that was one of his primary temperamental qualities: subtracting dialogue, substituting movement, images. Most days he did ten to 15 set-ups, sometimes as few as six or as many as 24. Some time was lost to bad weather on location, but Ford picked up three days during the studio portion of the shoot, and wrapped a week over schedule, at a cost of $2.5 million.

In his maturity Ford's preferred use of the camera was to put it in the right place and leave it there. Camera movement was limited; when he moved it, you noticed. So the rapid track-in to Ethan's face contorted with hate as he looks at a group of Indian captives, stands as an especially poignant reminder of the same track-in that Ford had used to introduce a boyish, optimistic John Wayne 17 years before. It's the same shot, but the actor and director have deepened over the years. The meaning of John Wayne has changed, and John Ford is the one who has changed it.

Ethan Edwards seethes with bitterness and rage. He mutilates corpses, behaves with the same ferocious cruelty as the Indians he despises. The years drift by, but Ethan just keeps coming. Ford here is making use of what David Thomson called "The way in which [John Wayne] could carry heroism so close to something terrible and ugly and solitary. Something not fit to come into the house." Ethan gives no quarter, not to anyone; he even mistreats Martin, his companion for the seven or so years that the film encompasses. Martin is part Indian, and therefore inferior.

Interestingly, the script for *The Searchers* does not open or close with doors, and the climax, in which Ethan confronts and transcends his racism and hatred, is quite different. In the script, after Ethan chases down Debbie, he holds a gun to her head. Because she has become the squaw of the man who killed her parents, she must die. "I'm sorry girl… shut your eyes," Ethan says. The camera tracks down Ethan's gun arm and moves into a close-up of Debbie's face, 'eyes gazing fearlessly, innocently into Ethan's.' The gun lowers. Ethan holsters the weapon and walks over to her. "You sure favour your mother," he says, extending his hand. She takes it, and he helps her to her feet.

ABOVE
Still from 'The Long Gray Line' (1955)
Martin Maher (Tyrone Power) romances Mary O'Donnell (Maureen O'Hara) in the true story of an instructor at West Point. As Martin reflects on whether his life was worth living, the film seems a little schizophrenic. On the one hand the film revels in the ritual of militarism, and on the other it regrets that the young men go off to war never to return.

PAGES 152/153
On the set of 'Mister Roberts' (1955)
Whilst filming on location at the Naval Air Base in Midway, Ford took a swing at Henry Fonda (right). Fonda wanted to keep exactly to the successful stage play in which he had starred for seven years and Ford wanted to make a Ford film. The rift meant that Ford and Fonda never made another picture together.

On the set of 'The Searchers' (1956)
John Wayne plays racist Ethan Edwards, who has a last-minute change of heart. Throughout the filming there was a seriousness and conviction in Wayne that others had not seen during the production of his other films. Harry Carey, Jr. said: "He didn't kid around on 'The Searchers' like he had on other shows. Ethan was always in his eyes."

This is all right, and it makes explicit that the reason Ethan cannot kill her is her resemblance to her dead mother, whom Ethan loved. But it lacks dynamism.

Ford loses the business and changes the dialogue. In a picturesque medium-long shot, Ethan stands over the cowering young woman, poised for murder, when he suddenly reaches down and hoists her over his head in one swooping movement, a gesture that repeats his greeting to the child Debbie in the beginning of the film. He brings her down to a cradle position and quietly murmurs "Let's go home, Debbie." The murderous Ethan finally feels the tidal pull of family; humanity is affirmed over hate and destruction.

In touching Debbie, he feels a human being rather than the abstraction of his racism.

As performed by John Wayne, it's one of the great moments in movies – emotionally true, murder alchemically transmuted into the protective embrace of love. Ford insists that we can only realize our truest selves when we can accept all of the many forms of humanity we meet.

Ford shot the final scene in the late afternoon. Ethan brings Debbie and Martin home, they dismount and walk through the doorway, leaving Ethan outside. "It just included a doorway," remembered John Wayne. "I was outside and they came in [from outside] and [moved past] the camera and turned around… It was emotional, and as they went in the door in the dark and got out of sight, and there was just me in the doorway and the wind blowing, I thought of Harry Carey. He had a stance where he put his left hand on his right arm. He did this incessantly.

"Well, when they took the little girl past the camera… Ollie [Carey] looked around at me, I just took the pose. The tears poured out of her eyes. It was a lovely dramatic moment in my life and I'm sure in hers."

The door closes, dooming Ethan Edwards to wander 'between the winds' for all eternity. Little more can be added to the tragedy of the hero.

The Searchers is a great film, but it is not without flaws; there is the strange, off-putting sequence of Look, Martin's Indian bride, an object of ridicule from the beginning, mostly because she's fat and sexually unattractive. Ford's treatment of Look feels brutal and unfunny, especially if, as is almost certainly the case, he thought of the sequence as comic relief. It's entirely possible that Ford felt he was working too close to the bone with *The Searchers*, that he felt there might be too much about racism, too much about miscegenation. The tension may have needed an outlet, but the comic interludes Ford devised – Look, Ken Curtis' Charlie McCorry – are too coarse by half.

The Searchers is Ford's most cogent statement on the conflict between civilization and wilderness, between freedom and responsibility, and most of it is expressed visually, by the juxtaposition of relentless figures in an isolated, tortured landscape. (Credit for the unusual clarity of the stunning images should go to Vistavision, by far the most visually sophisticated widescreen process of the period.)

As Stuart Byron would write, 'If the movie achieves epic status, it is because it says – with passionate and agonizing conviction – that the beliefs of both conservatives and liberals are equally valid: The American Dream is real and true, and yet America is a country founded on violence.'

Ethan embodies a complexity that is rare in the movies, rare even in literature. He hates Indians for their savagery *and* takes their scalps for killing his relatives; he despises Martin's Cherokee blood *and* makes him his heir; he wants to kill his niece for having sex with an Indian *and* he embraces her and takes her safely home. Ethan is a monster *and* he is John Wayne. 'Do I contradict myself?' asked Walt Whitman. 'Very well then I contradict myself, I am large, I contain multitudes.' So does Ethan Edwards. So does John Ford.

"He had an eye for the motion picture miracle. He could see the picture in his head. He could see the finished scene. And, once he got the actors on the set, he could see if it looked unrealistic, or staged, or not honest. And he wanted it honest, he wanted it spontaneous."

William Wellman, Jr.

Still from 'The Searchers' (1956)
Minister and Texas Ranger, Captain Reverend Samuel Johnson Clayton (Ward Bond, left) keeps his own counsel as Ethan Edwards (John Wayne) says goodbye to his brother's wife, Martha (Dorothy Jordan). Clayton sees Martha stroke Ethan's coat in private, and from this we divine that they love each other. Furthermore, it could be argued that Ethan's desire to kill the kidnapped girl Debbie is because she could be his daughter.

> "For Ford, Monument Valley was not only a location. It was his dream of the America he loved."

Martin Jurow

ABOVE
On the set of 'The Searchers' (1956)
Henry Brandon asked Ford why he cast him (a blue-eyed German actor) as Scar. Ford said "the exception, dramatically speaking, is always more exciting than the rule."

RIGHT
On the set of 'The Searchers' (1956)
In this sequence, Martin Pawley does not want to sleep with the Indian woman Look (Beulah Archuletta, in red to the right of the umbrella) so he kicks her out of bed. This is played for comic effect. She leaves and the next time we hear of her, she has been killed by the cavalry. Ford used comedy to counterpoint the real issue in this film, i.e. did Debbie have sex with Scar?

Going Home
1957–1973

The Searchers was the beginning of the final stage of Ford's career. Ford had never shot a lot of film, but now he began shooting even less, and with fewer set-ups. Ford began reducing his elements, narrowing the number of characters and sets, the better to concentrate on his themes. He lost interest in montage, in editing, and each shot became denser with emotion.

In a sense, the films become more theatrical; Monument Valley, for instance, becomes something of a natural proscenium, with buttes on either side of the screen and riders in deep focus on the horizon. Partly, this was a function of Ford's age – fewer set-ups meant less time in production, and less energy expended. But it was also a function of an older artist knowing what was essential about his art and letting the rest of it fall away.

In Ireland he directed an anthology film called *The Rising of the Moon* (1957), charming but basically an excuse for a trip back to the ancestral home. Then came *The Wings of Eagles* (1957), a biography of Ford's friend and occasional screenwriter Frank Wead that contains one of John Wayne's best performances – he even foregoes his toupee. Ward Bond does a funny turn as John Dodge (read 'John Ford'), a gruff Hollywood director with pictures of Harry Carey and Tom Mix on his walls. But Ford's tendency towards mythologizing meant that he could not bring himself to honestly portray the alcoholism of Wead's wife and their barren home life.

The film does have an odd undercurrent: Frank Wead is a man consumed by his profession, estranged from any domestic life, a virtual stranger to his children, unable to completely give himself to the wife who loves him, truly comfortable only with the less demanding company of men. The result is a perceptible sense of loss and incompletion that increases as he ages. Either Ford and Wead shared a remarkable number of character traits or Ford was lending him a lot of his own.

Ford returned to Europe for an odd little picture called *Gideon of Scotland Yard* (aka *Gideon's Day*, 1958), a police procedural with Jack Hawkins that clips along but carries no residual effect whatever and doesn't even look like a Ford film.

The Last Hurrah (1958) was an adaptation of a best-selling novel about a famous Mayor of Boston. With Spencer Tracy in the leading role, it seemed to be a natural subject for Ford. There's a good story, an omnipresent sense of loss, a strong leading man, a rogues' gallery of great character actors, but something is missing. Mainly, the dramatic lines are botched and there's no sense of place, of the city where all this

"He could be the nicest guy in the world, and he could be the meanest. You never knew which was going to happen. Ford was a fascinating man because he played a cat and mouse game. Sooner or later, he wanted to dominate you."

Winston Miller

is taking place. Ford reflexively sneers at nearly everybody younger than Mayor Frank Skeffington, all of whom are overplayed as air-headed idiots in the manner of a television sitcom, revealing a lack of sympathy with the modern world.

The director was now in his mid-60s, always a dangerous time for a film director, so much of whose business involves the expenditure of energy. Not only that, but Ford was having increasing trouble with his eyes; he had cataract surgery just after completing *Mogambo*, leaving him highly sensitive to light. Ford was now hurtling forward on momentum rather than desire, as was shown with *The Horse Soldiers* (1959), a Western cursed by bad decisions and malevolent fate. Ford was unable to establish a simpatico with co-star William Holden, and an already problematic script was rendered irrelevant when Fred Kennedy, one of Ford's favourite stuntmen, was killed on location doing a basic horse fall. It was nobody's fault, but Ford was devastated; he simply packed up and went home, leaving about 20 pages of location footage unshot.

Kennedy's death made Ford much more cautious about stunts; horse falls on Westerns became practically nonexistent, and he shut down his practical jokes and gags on the set. His age, combined with his caution, made the location footage of the films that followed *The Horse Soldiers* shorter as well as less vibrant than before.

Sergeant Rutledge (1960) is one of Ford's most interesting late pictures, a story of the Buffalo soldiers – the black soldiers of the Ninth and Tenth Cavalry, former slaves who tracked and fought but whose leadership was white. (The highest rank a Buffalo soldier could attain was First Sergeant.)

Warner Brothers wanted Sidney Poitier or Harry Belafonte as the star, but Ford said they weren't tough enough. He hired Woody Strode, a splendid physical specimen who had played football on the same UCLA team as Jackie Robinson and whose Hawaiian wife had gone to school with Pat and Barbara Ford.

The plot of *Sergeant Rutledge* – a teenage girl has been raped and killed on a frontier outpost, and her father, a major, has also been killed – has similarities with *To Kill a Mockingbird* (1962), with the commander of the Buffalo soldiers taking the place of Atticus Finch. Sergeant Braxton Rutledge is seen stumbling from the scene wounded and is presumed guilty until the court martial reveals the true killer. The strong story, the compression of the sets, Ford's ennobling exteriors, and the power of the theme carry the picture through.

It's a film of strong juxtapositions, and it's a courtroom *noir* as much as a Western – the expressionist light with which Ford photographs the murdered girl, the enormous inflammatory close-up of Woody Strode's hand over Constance Towers' face. Once again, Ford demonstrates his concern over racism; the unspoken devotion between the white lieutenant and his black troops is moving, as is the scene where Constance Towers cradles a wounded Buffalo soldier in her arms.

Two Rode Together (1961) has strong echoes of *The Searchers*: two ill-matched men (James Stewart and Richard Widmark) go after whites captured by a renegade part-Indian. But the film has a loose, jocular tone that doesn't fit with its theme; everything seems pitched a bit too high. The lighting is too bright, the actors are too broad and the voices are too loud. Unusually for Ford, the film feels physically slack – the images are largely recessive and uninteresting, and the locations are scrubby and lack definition. The entire picture feels like Ford is going through the motions.

Some of the same criticisms about an undistinguished physical production could be levelled at Ford's next film, but *The Man Who Shot Liberty Valance* (1962) had one of the most remarkable scripts of Ford's career. Although colour had become standard in the industry, Ford insisted that the film be shot in black and white

ABOVE
Still from 'The Rising of the Moon' (1957)
In 'A Minute's Wait', a goat replaces the Frobishers (Michael Trubshawe and Anita Sharp Bolster) in their first-class compartment.

OPPOSITE TOP
Still from 'Gideon of Scotland Yard' (1958)
We follow a day in the life on Inspector George Gideon (Jack Hawkins) as his duty to work takes precedence over his personal life.

OPPOSITE BOTTOM LEFT
On the set of 'The Colter Craven Story' (1960)
Ford shot this episode of Ward Bond's TV show 'Wagon Train' in six days, and had John Wayne cameo as General Sherman, but Bond died before it was aired on 23 November 1960.

OPPOSITE BOTTOM RIGHT
Still from 'The Last Hurrah' (1958)
Frank Skeffington (Spencer Tracy) was a wise, humorous, melancholy political leader in the tradition of Ford's Abe Lincoln and Judge Priest.

ABOVE
On the set of 'The Horse Soldiers' (1959)
John Ford (centre) shows Constance Towers how to punch John Wayne.

LEFT
Still from 'The Horse Soldiers' (1959)
Towers connects with Wayne in a cut scene. Set during the American Civil War, the story was based on Colonel Benjamin H. Grierson's 600-mile raid into Confederate territory to destroy railway supply lines and to distract Confederate troops whilst General Ulysses S. Grant drove towards Vicksburg. Ford was a Civil War buff and made sure that everything was as authentic as possible. However, Ford stopped shooting after the death of veteran stuntman Fred Kennedy during a routine stunt, leaving the film with a rather short, uncertain ending.

Still from 'Sergeant Rutledge' (1960)
In the opening scenes, Sergeant Braxton
Rutledge (Woody Strode), who is on the run for
murdering and raping Lucy Dabney and then
killing her father, saves Mary Beecher
(Constance Towers) from marauding Apaches.
This powerful courtroom drama shows Rutledge
being accused because of the colour of his skin,
a reflection of prevailing attitudes to blacks in
1960s America.

On the set of 'Two Rode Together' (1961)
John Ford (right) said that this was "the worst piece of crap I've done in twenty years." It is almost as if Ford were mocking 'The Searchers' with James Stewart (left) and Richard Widmark looking for white captives.

because of the key scene of the gunfight in the dark street. Once the sequence was edited, he said to cameraman William Clothier, "See, you got a damn good sequence out of that. It wouldn't have been half as good in colour."

The Man Who Shot Liberty Valance is a memory play, from its under-populated sets to the archetypes of its characters. Landscape is almost completely absent, and Ford's eye for composition is muted – visually, it's among the most ordinary of his movies. But the thematic resonance more than compensates for the fact that it's an old man's movie – not the expansive symphony of *Stagecoach* or *The Searchers*, but a muted chamber piece.

A sweet gallantry had been a keynote quality of Ford's ever since *Straight Shooting*, but *The Man Who Shot Liberty Valance* overwhelms that with sadness. In movies as disparate as *The Grapes of Wrath*, *My Darling Clementine* and *The Searchers*, Ford had nudged his characters toward a final ascendance to myth; now, he begins the film with the myth and methodically deconstructs it on the way to a mournful irony, utterly undercutting the newspaperman's aphorism that became famous: "When the legend becomes fact, print the legend."

There is an odd passivity at the heart of the characters. Tom Doniphon (John Wayne) lets Ranse Stoddard (James Stewart) have his woman Hallie (Vera Miles), his town, his West. As for Stoddard, he is powerless before the demonic outlaw Liberty Valance, and powerless before Doniphon.

The only true agent of power is time, and it does terrible things – the gap between the firmly idealistic, younger Stoddard and the self-obsessed windbag he becomes is heartbreaking. In the end, Stoddard, Hallie and the few remaining characters are all haunted, and everything is changed, changed utterly, except for the desert. Everybody gets what they thought they wanted, but nobody is happy. Welcome to the 20th century.

If, as Scott Fitzgerald said, the mark of a first-rate intelligence is the ability to hold two contradictory ideas in your head at the same time, then Ford had a first-rate intelligence. For Ford, every triumph carries the embryo of eventual failure. In *The Searchers*, as well as *The Man Who Shot Liberty Valance*, the kind of men needed to master the wilderness are the kind of men that must be expelled by the civilization they help to create. If society is to benefit from someone's sacrifice, legend must take precedence over truth. Ford celebrates America's history and values, but he also articulates the contradictions that can lead to a mournful pessimism. Ford is too

OPPOSITE TOP
Still from 'The Man Who Shot Liberty Valance' (1962)
There is an underlying disenchantment with the mythology of the Western in many of Ford's later films. He had always opposed the hypocrisy of society, and his poetic outcasts comment upon it. As Ford got older, the outcasts became more bitter and cynical. Something had gone wrong. This is highlighted in Ford's last masterpiece, where pacifist and politician Ranse Stoddard (James Stewart, right) runs for office on the lie that he shot Liberty Valance, when it was in fact his friend Tom Doniphon (John Wayne). At the end, Stoddard's shameful secret will not be revealed because the newspapers want to print the legend, but as Peter Bogdanovich points out, Ford showed the facts.

OPPOSITE BOTTOM
Still from 'How the West Was Won' (1962)
Zeb (George Peppard) leaves home to fight for glory in the American Civil War. However, after viewing the dead bodies at Shiloh Zeb says, "There ain't much glory in lookin' at a man with his guts hangin' out."

BELOW
On the set of 'How the West Was Won' (1962)
Ford directs Carroll Baker as George Peppard and Claude Johnson wait behind him. Andy Devine, dressed in Civil War uniform is behind the huge Cinerama camera. Ford framed his shots very precisely so that the doors and fences helped to mask the lines between the three Cinerama panels.

complex an artist to believe that the modern world is a 180-degree betrayal of the
past; rather, he believes that history is organic and the present is the logical
extension of the past.

Like many Ford films, *The Man Who Shot Liberty Valance* focuses on the need to
subordinate individual will to a collective struggle for a greater good; unlike many
Ford films, it overtly questions whether the sacrifice is justified. It deftly shows the
ragged process by which stories become legends, and legends become history.

In the end, Stoddard and his wife are once again on the train. "Look at it," she
says, looking out the window. "It was once a wilderness; now it's a garden. Aren't
you proud?"

"Hallie," replies Stoddard, "Who put the cactus rose on Tom's coffin?"
"I did."

The two sit, lost in contemplation. The conductor breaks their reverie and speaks
the film's final words: "Nothing's too good for the man who shot Liberty Valance."
Just as Stoddard has pretended to be the man who shot Liberty Valance, his wife has
pretended to love her husband more than she loves Tom Doniphon. Each has paid a
price we can only imagine. As the train recedes across a landscape, Ford's bleakest
film ends with a poignant dying fall.

A lessening of energy had been evident in Ford's work for some time, but the
meditative complexity of a script like *The Man Who Shot Liberty Valance*
compensated. But it would prove to be Ford's last masterpiece, as well as his last
financial success. The films he made after that were, with one exception, unusually

ambitious for a director at the tail end of their career, but Ford was unable to summon the creative or physical energies to make them come alive.

If Ford disliked CinemaScope, Cinerama must have been a waking nightmare. Close-ups were impossible. But he managed to give his episode of *How the West Was Won* (1962), shot in 14 days in the middle of 1961, a pleasing intimacy, a sense of eavesdropping on history, as John Wayne's Sherman and Harry Morgan's U. S. Grant wrangle about the Civil War.

Donovan's Reef (1963) was a coarsened reimagining of *The Quiet Man*, in which even John Wayne realized he was miscast. "I was too old," he said. But the fact of the matter was that it was not a script that Ford would have been able to get financed without Wayne's participation. The locations in Hawaii and the presence of the *Araner* – in the film's opening scenes – provide most of the pleasures to be had.

Cheyenne Autumn (1964) was a noble attempt to portray the Trail of Tears from the inside, but the nearly three-hour epic proved one of Ford's most misguided films, hopelessly enervated, with a cast of various ethnicities (Mexican, Italian) playing Indians.

Young Cassidy (1965) was potentially the richest of the late films, a bio-drama about the great Irish playwright Sean O'Casey. Ford was an exceedingly well-read and discerning critic of Irish literature, and was friends with Liam O'Flaherty as well as O'Casey. He assembled a powerhouse cast: Maggie Smith, Julie Christie, Michael Redgrave, Edith Evans, and Rod Taylor as Young Sean (Cassidy) O'Casey. O'Casey had written six volumes of autobiography – self-dramatization is bred in the bones

On the set of 'Donovan's Reef' (1963)
Set on the South Pacific island of Haleakaloha, this film is probably the purest distillation of all of Ford's thematic quirks. Racism. Hypocrisy. Religion. Drinking. Fighting. Dancing. Ritual. Family. Eating. All the opposing forces eventually reach a compromise, an equilibrium. In this picture we see Ford's beloved ketch, the 'Araner', which was used in the film.

"I like animals, and then, after baseball, I like people."

John Ford

of the Irish – and even did some dialogue work on the screenplay himself. Ford liked the script a great deal, but shortly after production began in Ireland he began drinking at night. Rod Taylor, starring in the film, remembered that "the hangovers must have been, at his age, monumental. But his mind was clear and creative. He knew what he wanted and if something better happened, he'd print it and go away. His favourite phrase to me was, 'There are no problems, only opportunities.' I've kept that slogan ever since I met him."

Ford left the picture after three weeks. It was completed by the great cameraman Jack Cardiff, and largely feels like a Ford film, although the dramatic trajectory is truncated by script alterations. Even then, it's Ford's best picture after *The Man Who Shot Liberty Valance*. The Easter uprising seems to take place on one street, but the film soon finds its rhythm, helped along by Julie Christie's vivid carnal charge. The scene of O'Casey having to bargain with the morticians over his mother's corpse nicely captures the meanness of aspects of Irish life, as well as some of O'Casey's contempt for his own people.

7 Women (1966), Ford's last picture, was ambitious, but it was also hopelessly anachronistic. The story of a group of missionaries on a backlot China menaced by a warlord played by Mike Mazurki, might just have passed muster around 1939, with, say, Katharine Hepburn in the part played by Anne Bancroft, but there was little critical or audience interest in such a story in 1966.

Three successive financial and critical failures might be endured by a young director, but an old director has little hope of maintaining a career in such circumstances, especially when his health is shaky. For the last years of his life Ford chafed under the entirely unaccustomed weight of unemployment.

He kept his hand in by working on a documentary about his friend Louis "Chesty" Puller (*Chesty* was released in 1976), and functioning as executive producer for a government documentary entitled *Vietnam! Vietnam!* (1971). The decorated commander of World War Two had no sympathy with protests against the war in Vietnam, although Ford didn't pretend to understand the war itself. The excesses of the war protests nudged him to the right, and he became a Nixon supporter. (Ford's politics had been straight left during the 1930s and during World War Two, although he voted for Dwight Eisenhower in the 1950s because of his knowledge of and affection for the man due to their shared experiences during the war. It was back to the Democratic – and the Irish – column in 1960, for John Kennedy.)

If Hollywood, at long last, had no more use for John Ford, there was the younger generation of critics and the government. Peter Bogdanovich's book-length interview was published in 1967, and Ford bought two copies, although if anybody asked him he would claim it was "filled with inaccuracies". He entered the twilight world of the director who is too old to work, a world of tributes, interviews and making the rounds of film festivals to collect awards. But Ford was not a man who enjoyed that sort of thing. "He wasn't bitter," remembered his friend, the director Burt Kennedy. "He was angry."

In January 1969, the clubhouse at the Field Photo Farm was destroyed by fire. A few months later, Ford donated the land and the remaining buildings to the Motion Picture Television and Relief Fund. The chapel was moved to the Motion Picture Home, where it still stands, and the land itself was sold by the fund for $276,825. Ford's most remarkable *beau geste* was no more. Shortly thereafter, he sold the *Araner*.

OPPOSITE TOP
Still from 'Cheyenne Autumn' (1964)
The Cheyenne nation is reduced to 286 and they decide to undertake a 1500-mile trip to their ancestral homelands in Dakota. The running joke among the Navajo, who also played Apaches, Sioux and Arapaho in Ford's films, is that they always answered the white man in Navajo, and that it would often be insulting, referring to the size of the Colonel's penis, or the fact that the white man crawled on his stomach like a snake. Consequently, screenings of Ford's films for the Navajo were often filled with laughter.

OPPOSITE BOTTOM
On the set of 'Cheyenne Autumn' (1964)
As with the romance between Lt. Tom Cantrell and Mary Beecher in 'Sergeant Rutledge', the romance between Captain Archer and Deborah Wright (Carroll Baker) distracts from, and ultimately hurts, the main plotline.

PAGES 174/175
On the set of 'Cheyenne Autumn' (1964)
After 'The Horse Soldiers', Ford never asked his stunt men to perform dangerous stunts. However, Ford always stayed close to the action, by the camera, as he had done on 'The Iron Horse' (page 55) and 'The Wings of Eagles' (page 13). This picture shows a stunt sequence being filmed by two cameras. Ford is in his usual position, sitting under the left camera, wearing a white hat.

A few times he was lured to UCLA to speak to film students. "Anybody can direct a picture once they know the fundamentals," he told them. "Directing is not a mystery, not an art. The main thing about motion pictures is: photograph the people's eyes. Photograph their eyes…

"Forget about the camera. Get a good cameraman – he knows more about a camera than you'll ever know… work with your people. Look at their faces. See their eyes." He never used the term "movies" or even "films." It was always "pictures." Like Fitzgerald's Monroe Stahr, he was just making pictures, images that told a story, communicated a mood.

In October 1970, Ford tripped over some laundry on his back patio and broke his left hip. He was hospitalized for over a month. In September 1971, he was diagnosed with cancer and was offered two treatment options: aggressive surgery or chemotherapy. "Cut it out," he snapped. "Let's go for it." The operation revealed an inoperable malignancy; his condition was terminal. In 1973, he was honoured with the first Life Achievement award from the American Film Institute. Visibly suffering from the effects of the cancer, Ford was emaciated and barely able to stand from the wheelchair pushed by John Wayne. It was clearly the great director's last hurrah.

Toward the end, he spent almost all of his time in bed, watching television, taking his meals off TV trays. Friends came to visit and say goodbye: George Cukor, Burt Kennedy, Woody Strode, Lindsay Anderson, Howard Hawks, Budd Boetticher, John Wayne. The man the world knew as John Ford died at 6:35 p.m. on 31 August 1973. Woody Strode, Pat Ford and Ford's sister draped an American flag over his body, drank a toast to his life with a glass of brandy, then broke the glasses. At Holy Cross cemetery, Ford was buried a few feet away from his brother Frank.

Tributes from his peers poured in but the tribute that would have meant the most to Ford is the way that his work has maintained its hold on the imagination of the audience. Ford's vision of America became America's vision of itself, and the world's. In Monument Valley, Goulding's Lodge is thronged by tourists from all over the world, drawn to a small trading post in the middle of nowhere by the incantatory and mysterious power of images made more than a half-century ago.

John Ford was a magnificent piece of work, but no simple hero – he was grander, tougher and sadder than any hero can allow himself to be. He was clever and he was ruthless. It was not his nature to trust, but to test. Beneath the often scary surface, he was a mushy sentimentalist, and beneath that was the hard, selfish core of the true artist.

He cared nothing for money, little for politics, cared a great deal about tradition and character. He believed in America and he believed in the future, even as he mourned the past. Ethan Edwards leaves his feelings for his brother's wife unstated because it would destroy the family; Tom Doniphon lets Ranse Stoddard have the girl he loves because he's smart enough to know the lawyer can offer her a world Doniphon can only dream about and wouldn't want anyway. Always, Ford lingered over the man deserted by time and tide, because he knew it happens to everybody – even famous film directors.

If Ford had never made *The Searchers* or, for that matter, any other Western, he would still be a major director, with a gift for repose and an astringent wisdom. But Ford's Westerns gave the genre a vision and, in Monument Valley, a signature. No other place evokes the West so unambiguously. While the Western would still have a history without Ford, it would be nowhere near as glorious.

Still from '7 Women' (1966)
An atheistic doctor (Anne Bancroft, sitting) sacrifices herself to save the other women and a newborn baby at the mission.

"He had a strange, old world quality with women. He was always very courteous with them. If you used bad language in front of women, he'd throw you right off the set."

Frank Baker

Ultimately, Ford's greatest gift was his ability to combine the epic with the intimate – not just in the same film, but in the same moment, the personal moving side by side with the mythological.

The work of this wild colonial boy flared with a moral imagination equal to the melancholy that marked his life. His instinctive knowledge that things usually end in defeat balanced his idealism and sentimentality. Ford gave the world an America that was a lived experience, a history that can be used. John Ford's history became the history of his time, mirroring it, transfiguring it, explaining America to itself. He devised an often belligerent, deceitful carapace to protect an inner man on the run from insoluble inner tensions, largely revolving around the gap between what he really wanted to be – a naval hero – and what he actually was – a poet. Like Ethan Edwards, he drove all before him with the force of his fierce personality.

John Ford's films are about the search for a place we can never find, and form an album of America as it was meant to have been, as well as of the place it really is. His films have the power to burn through space to a place inside us, an art about memory that makes our own lives more vivid.

ABOVE
Still from 'The American West of John Ford' (1971)
John Wayne and John Ford reunited in Monument Valley for a sequence of this documentary.

PAGES 178/179
Monument Valley
One of John Ford's favourite places to shoot the valley was named Ford Point by the Indians. George Stevens, director of 'Shane' and 'Giant', once visited Monument Valley on a location scout and went everywhere with his view finder. He gave up and returned to Hollywood. "All I could see," he explained, "Were 'John Ford' shots."

"I've always thought I was abrupt, but never rude."

John Ford

Chronology

ABOVE
Family photo
John and Mary Ford with their children Patrick and Barbara.

RIGHT
On the set of 'Young Mr. Lincoln' (1939)
Henry Fonda closes his eyes for a moment while John Ford (left) instructs his crew.

OPPOSITE
On the set of 'The Man Who Shot Liberty Valance' (1962)
James Stewart, John Ford and John Wayne.

1894 Birth of John Martin Feeney on 1 February, to John and Barbara Curran Feeney in Cape Elizabeth, Maine. His father is a bartender, storekeeper and occasional functionary in the Democratic Party.

1906 Young John Feeney comes down with diphtheria. While recuperating, his sister Maime reads to him *Treasure Island*, *Tom Sawyer* and *Huckleberry Finn* among others. He promptly falls in love with narrative, and with reading.

1912 Earns second string fullback status on the Portland High football team.

1913 Starting fullback on the Portland High football team that wins the state championship. Becomes known to his classmates as "Bull" Feeney for the way he hits the line.

1914 Graduates from high school on 18 June, with an 84.9 average and three football letters. Spends his summer vacation in Los Angeles with his big brother Frank, an actor and director under the name Francis Ford. Goes to work for his brother, and adopts the name Ford to take advantage of whatever nepotistic connections can be made.

1915–16 Works as assistant director, prop man and occasional actor for his brother Frank at Universal.

1917 Directs and stars in his first film, a two-reeler called *The Tornado*, released 3 March. Five more shorts follow before the 27 August release of his first full-length feature, *Straight Shooting*. Three more features are released before the end of the year.

1920 At a St. Patrick's Day party thrown by the director Rex Ingram, Ford meets a nurse named Mary McBryde

Smith, who has come to California to visit her brother. They marry on 3 July. In December, Ford leaves Universal and signs with Fox, where he will remain, with frequent loan-outs, until 1946.

1921 Birth of Ford's son Patrick Michael Roper Ford on 3 April.

1922 Birth of Ford's daughter Barbara Nugent Ford on 16 December.

1924 Release of *The Iron Horse*, Ford's first big-budget, mass-audience hit, on 28 August. A budget of $280,000 returned over $2 million in the first year.

1931 Loaned out to Sam Goldwyn to direct *Arrowsmith*. Does not get along with Ronald Colman or Goldwyn, goes on a binge and is removed from the picture in its final stages. The film is among the year's top 20 earners.

1935 Release of *The Informer*, a great critical and modest commercial success that wins Ford his first Best Director Oscar.

1936–37 Affair with Katharine Hepburn. Ultimately, Ford refuses to leave his wife and the affair ends, although the two remain friendly for the rest of Ford's life.

1939 Release of *Stagecoach*, which revitalizes the Western genre.

1940–41 Release of *The Grapes of Wrath* and *How Green Was My Valley*, winning Ford back-to-back Oscars for Best Director. Also directs *The Long Voyage Home*,

based on four one-act plays by Eugene O'Neill. It is the first production of Argosy Films, the independent company Ford sets up with producer Merian C. Cooper.

1942–44 Service in the Navy during World War Two, running the Field Photo Service, providing visual documentation for military planning, as well as supervising propaganda releases. Re-edits *December 7th* and photographs and directs *The Battle of Midway*, winning another Academy Award for the latter.

1945 Begins directing *They Were Expendable* in February, on leave from the Navy. The Field Photographic Unit is officially disbanded on 27 September; a day later, Ford is released from active duty, having attained the rank of Commander.

1946 *My Darling Clementine*, a highly personal take on Wyatt Earp and the gunfight at the OK Corral, returns Ford to Monument Valley for the first time since *Stagecoach*.

1947 *The Fugitive*, an adaptation of Graham Greene's *The Power and the Glory*, fails critically and commercially, putting Argosy Productions in a financial hole. Ford commits to a series of westerns as a means of returning the company to solvency.

1948 *Fort Apache, 3 Godfathers*.

1949 *She Wore a Yellow Ribbon*

1950 *Wagon Master, Rio Grande*

1951 Ford is promoted to the rank of rear Admiral in the Naval Reserve.

1952 *The Quiet Man*, a commercial and critical hit, wins Ford his last Best Director Oscar.

1953 *Mogambo* takes $5.2 million in America, making it Ford's biggest grosser.

1955 Directs location photography for *Mister Roberts*, during which he engages in a fistfight with Henry Fonda. Begins drinking and is forced to leave the picture when his gall bladder has to be removed. Mervyn LeRoy completes the picture.

1956 *The Searchers*, posterity's consensus nomination for the greatest Ford film of all.

1960 Ford makes *Sergeant Rutledge*, his film about the all-black units of the U.S. Cavalry known as the Buffalo Soldiers. Also shoots much second (and first) unit footage for John Wayne's production of *The Alamo*.

1962 *The Man Who Shot Liberty Valance*, Ford's last great film, is released.

1963 *Donovan's Reef*, the last collaboration with John Wayne, which also provides a good glimpse of Ford's yacht, the *Araner* – his primary getaway vehicle for the last 35 years of his life.

1964 *Cheyenne Autumn*, planned as Ford's farewell to the Western as well as to Monument Valley, emerges as a severe disappointment.

1965 Ford leaves *Young Cassidy*, an ambitious biographical film about Sean O'Casey, after several weeks of production. Jack Cardiff completes the picture.

1966 *7 Women*, Ford's last film, a commercial and critical disaster. He is now, for all intents and purposes, retired, although not happily.

1970 *Chesty: A Tribute to a Legend*, a documentary about Lewis "Chesty" Puller, the most decorated Marine in history.

1971 *Vietnam! Vietnam!*, a documentary produced by the government, on which Ford serves as executive producer/consultant, is barely released. *Directed by John Ford*, Peter Bogdanovich's loving documentary about the man and his work, is released.

1973 Ford is awarded the first Life Achievement Award from the American Film Institute on 31 March. Already suffering from the abdominal cancer that will kill him, he spends most of the evening in a wheelchair, until he rises to accept the award and salute President Richard M. Nixon, who confers on him the rank of Admiral for the night. Death of John Ford from cancer, on 31 August.

Filmography

The Tornado (1917)
Crew: *Director/Screenplay* Jack Ford, two reels, presumed lost.
Cast: Jack Ford (Jack Dayton), Jean Hathaway (His Irish mother), John Duffy (Slick).

The Trail of Hate (1917)
Crew: *Director/Screenplay* Jack Ford, two reels, presumed lost.
Cast: Jack Ford (Lt. Jack Brewer), Duke Worne (Capt. Dana Holden), Louise Granville (Madge).

The Scrapper (1917)
Crew: *Director/Screenplay* Jack Ford, *Photography* Ben Reynolds, two reels, presumed lost.
Cast: Jack Ford (Buck), Louise Granville (Helen), Duke Worne (Jerry).

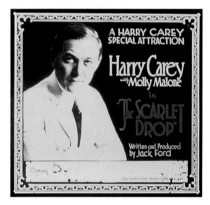

The Soul Herder (The Sky Pilot, 1917)
Crew: *Director* Jack Ford, *Screenplay* George Hively, *Photography* Ben Reynolds, three reels, presumed lost.
Cast: Harry Carey (Cheyenne Harry), Jean Hersholt (the Minister), Elizabeth James (his daughter).

Red Saunders Plays Cupid (1917)
Crew: *Director* Jack Ford, short film, presumed lost.
Cast: Harry Carey, Claire du Brey, George Webb, Rex De Rosselli.

Cheyenne's Pal (1917)
Crew: *Director/Story* Jack Ford, *Screenplay* Charles F. Wilson, Jr., *Photography* Fred F. Baker, two reels, presumed lost.
Cast: Harry Carey (Cheyenne Harry), Jim Corey (Jim), Gertrude Astor (dancehall girl).

Straight Shooting (1917)
Crew: *Director* Jack Ford, *Screenplay* George Hively, *Photography* George Scott, five reels.
Cast: Harry Carey (Cheyenne Harry), Molly Malone (Joan), Duke Lee (Thunder), Hoot Gibson (Danny).

The Secret Man (1917)
Crew: *Director* Jack Ford, *Screenplay* George Hively, *Photography* Ben Reynolds, five reels, only two reels exist.
Cast: Harry Carey (Cheyenne Harry), Morris Foster (Beauford), Vester Pegg (Sheriff).

A Marked Man (1917)
Crew: *Director/Story* Jack Ford, *Screenplay* George Hively, *Photography* John Brown, five reels, presumed lost.
Cast: Harry Carey (Cheyenne Harry), Molly Malone (Molly), Vester Pegg (Kent).

Bucking Broadway (1917)
Crew: *Director* Jack Ford, *Screenplay* George Hively, *Photography* John Brown, five reels.
Cast: Harry Carey (Cheyenne Harry), Molly Malone (Helen), L.M. Wells (Ben Clayton).

The Phantom Riders (1918)
Crew: *Director* Jack Ford, *Screenplay* George Hively, *Story* Henry McRae, *Photography* John Brown, five reels, presumed lost.
Cast: Harry Carey (Cheyenne Harry), Molly Malone (Molly), Buck Conners (her father).

Wild Women (1918)
Crew: *Director* Jack Ford, *Screenplay* George Hively, *Photography* John Brown, five reels, presumed lost.
Cast: Harry Carey (Cheyenne Harry), Molly Malone (The Princess), Martha Mattox (The Queen.).

Thieves Gold (1918)
Crew: *Director* Jack Ford, *Screenplay* George Hively, *Story* Frederic R. Bechdolt, *Photography* John Brown, five reels, presumed lost.
Cast: Harry Carey (Cheyenne Harry), Molly Malone (Alice), L.M. Wells (Savage).

The Scarlet Drop (Civil War Days, 1918)
Crew: *Director/Story* Jack Ford, *Screenplay* George Hively, *Photography* Ben Reynolds, five reels, 32 minutes still exists.
Cast: Harry Carey ('Kaintuck' Harry Ridge), Molly Malone (Molly), Vester Pegg (Calvert).

Hell Bent (The Three Bad Men, 1918)
Crew: *Director* Jack Ford, *Screenplay* Jack Ford, Harry Carey, *Photography* Ben Reynolds, 5,700 feet.
Cast: Harry Carey (Cheyenne Harry), Neva Gerber (Bess), Duke Lee (Cimarron Bill).

A Woman's Fool (1918)
Crew: *Director* Jack Ford, *Screenplay* George Hively, *Novel* Owen Wister, *Photography* Ben Reynolds, 60 minutes, presumed lost.
Cast: Harry Carey (Lin McLean), Betty Schade (Katie), Molly Malone (Jessie).

Three Mounted Men (1918)
Crew: *Director* Jack Ford, *Screenplay* Eugene B. Lewis, *Photography* Jack Brown, six reels, presumed lost.
Cast: Harry Carey (Cheyenne Harry), Joe Harris (Buck), Neva Gerber (Lola).

Roped (1919)
Crew: *Director* Jack Ford, *Screenplay* Eugene B. Lewis, *Photography* John Brown, six reels, presumed lost.
Cast: Harry Carey (Cheyenne Harry), Neva Gerber (Aileen), J. Farrell MacDonald (Butler).

The Fighting Brothers (His Buddy, 1919)
Crew: *Director* Jack Ford, *Screenplay* George Hively, *Story* George Hull, *Photography* John Brown, two reels, presumed lost.
Cast: Pete Morrison (Sheriff), Hoot Gibson (Lonnie), Yvette Mitchell (Conchita).

A Fight for Love (1919)
Crew: *Director* Jack Ford, *Screenplay* Eugene Lewis, *Photography* John Brown, six reels, presumed lost.
Cast: Harry Carey (Cheyenne Harry), Joe Harris (Black Michael), Neva Gerber (Katie).

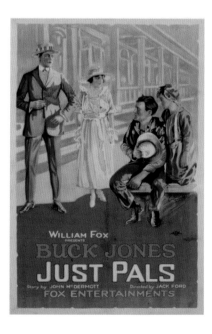

By Indian Post *(The Love Letter, 1919)*

Crew: *Director* Jack Ford. *Screenplay* H. Tipton Steck, *Story* William Wallace Cook, two reels.
Cast: Pete Morrison (Jode), Duke Lee (Pa), Magda Lane (Peg).

The Rustlers *(1919)*

Crew: *Director* Jack Ford, *Screenplay* George Hively, *Photography* John Brown, two reels, presumed lost.
Cast: Pete Morrison (Ben), Helen Gibson (Nell), Hoot Gibson (Deputy).

Bare Fists *(1919)*

Crew: *Director* Jack Ford, *Screenplay* Eugene B. Lewis, *Story* Bernard McConville. *Photography* John Brown, 5,500 feet, presumed lost.
Cast: Harry Carey (Cheyenne Harry), Molly McConnell (his mother), Joseph Girard (his father).

Gun Law *(The Posse's Prey, 1919)*

Crew: *Director* Jack Ford, *Screenplay* H. Tipton Steck, *Photography* John Brown, two reels, presumed lost.
Cast: Pete Morrison (Dick), Hoot Gibson (Bart), Helen Gibson (Letty).

The Gun Packer *(Old Wyoming Way, 1919)*

Crew: *Director* Jack Ford, *Screenplay* Karl Coolidge, *Story* Jack Ford, Harry Carey, *Photography* John Brown, two reels, presumed lost.
Cast: Ed Jones (Sandy), Pete Morrison (Pearl Handle), Magda Lane (Rose), Hoot Gibson (outlaw).

Riders of Vengeance *(1919)*

Crew: *Director* Jack Ford, *Screenplay* Jack Ford, Harry Carey, *Photography* John Brown, six reels, presumed lost.
Cast: Harry Carey (Cheyenne Harry), Seena Owen (the girl), J. Farrell MacDonald (Buell).

The Last Outlaw *(1919)*

Crew: *Director* Jack Ford, *Screenplay* H. Tipton Steck, *Story* Evelyne Campbell, *Photography* John Brown, two reels, one reel exists.
Cast: Ed Jones (Bud Coburn), Richard Cumming (Sheriff), Lucille Hutton (Idaleen).

The Outcasts of Poker Flat *(1919)*

Crew: *Director* Jack Ford, *Screenplay* H. Tipton Steck, *Stories* Bret Harte, *Photography* John Brown, six reels, presumed lost.
Cast: Harry Carey (Oakhurst), Cullen Landis (Tommy), Gloria Hope (Sophy).

Ace of the Saddle *(1919)*

Crew: *Director* Jack Ford, *Screenplay* George Hively, *Story* Frederick J. Jackson, *Photography* John Brown, six reels, presumed lost.
Cast: Harry Carey (Cheyenne Harry), Joe Harris (Sheriff), Duke Lee (Sheriff), Viola Barry (Madeline).

Rider of the Law *(Jim of the Rangers, 1919)*

Crew: *Director* Jack Ford, *Screenplay* H. Tipton Steck, *Story* G.B. Lancaster, *Photography* John Brown, five reels, presumed lost.

Cast: Harry Carey (Jim Kyneton), Gloria Hope (Betty), Vester Pegg (Nick).

A Gun Fightin' Gentleman *(1919)*

Crew: *Director* Jack Ford, *Screenplay* Hal Hoadley, *Story* Jack Ford, Harry Carey, *Photography* John Brown, five reels, three reels exist.
Cast: Harry Carey (Cheyenne Harry), J. Barney Sherry (John Merritt), Kathleen O'Connor (Helen).

Marked Men (1919)
Crew: *Director* Jack Ford, ***Screenplay*** H. Tipton Steck, ***Story*** Peter B. Kyne, ***Photography*** John Brown, five reels, presumed lost.
Cast: Harry Carey (Cheyenne Harry), J. Farrell MacDonald (Tom), Winifred Westover (Ruby).

The Prince of Avenue A (1920)
Crew: *Director* Jack Ford, ***Screenplay*** Charles J. Wilson, ***Story*** Charles and Frank Dazey, ***Photography*** John Brown, five reels, presumed lost.
Cast: James J. 'Gentleman Jim' Corbett (O'Connor), Mary Warren (Mary), Harry Northrup (Edgar).

The Girl in Number 29 (1920)
Crew: *Director* Jack Ford, ***Screenplay*** Philip Hurn, ***Story*** Elizabeth Jordan, ***Photography*** John Brown, five reels, presumed lost.
Cast: Frank Mayo (Devon), Harry Hilliard (Rodney), Elinor Fair (Barbara Devon).

Hitchin' Posts (1920)
Crew: *Director* Jack Ford, ***Screenplay*** George C. Hull, ***Story*** Harold Schumate, ***Photography*** Benjamin Kline, five reels, presumed lost.
Cast: Frank Mayo (Todd), Beatrice Burnham (Barbara Brereton), J. Farrell MacDonald (Joe).

Just Pals (1920)
Crew: *Director* Jack Ford, ***Screenplay*** Paul Schofield, ***Story*** John McDermott, ***Photography*** George Schneiderman, five reels.
Cast: Buck Jones (Bim), Helen Ferguson (Mary), George E. Stone (Bill).

The Big Punch (1921)
Crew: *Director* Jack Ford, ***Screenplay*** Jack Ford, Jules Furthman, ***Story*** Furthman, ***Photography*** Jack Good, five reels, presumed lost.
Cast: Buck Jones (Buck), Barbara Bedford (Hope), George Siegmann (Flash).

The Freeze Out (1921)
Crew: *Director* Jack Ford, ***Screenplay*** George C. Hull, ***Photography*** Harry C. Fowler, 4,400 feet, presumed lost.
Cast: Harry Carey (Ohio), Helen Ferguson (Zoe), Joe Harris (Headlight).

The Wallop (1921)
Crew: *Director* Jack Ford, ***Screenplay*** George C. Hull, ***Story*** Eugene Manlove Rhodes, ***Photography*** Harry C. Fowler, five reels, presumed lost.
Cast: Harry Carey (John Pringle), Joe Harris (Barela), J. Farrell MacDonald (Neuces River).

Desperate Trails (1921)
Crew: *Director* Jack Ford, ***Screenplay*** Elliott Clawson, ***Story*** Courtney Riley Cooper, ***Photography*** Harry Fowler, Robert DeGrasse, five reels, presumed lost.
Cast: Harry Carey (Carson), Irene Rich (Mrs Walker), George E. Stone (Danny Boy).

Action (Let's Go, 1921)
Crew: *Director* Jack Ford, ***Screenplay*** Harvey Gates, ***Story*** J. Allan Dunn, ***Photography*** John Brown, five reels.
Cast: Hoot Gibson (Sandy), Francis Ford (Soda Water), J. Farrell MacDonald (Mormon Peters).

Sure Fire (1921)
Crew: *Director* Jack Ford, ***Screenplay*** George Hull, ***Story*** Eugene Manlove Rhodes, ***Photography*** Virgil Miller, five reels, presumed lost.
Cast: Hoot Gibson (Jeff), Molly Malone (Marian), Reeves Eason (Sonny).

Jackie (1921)
Crew: *Director* Jack Ford, ***Screenplay*** Dorothy Yost, ***Story*** Marguerite Evans, ***Photography*** Georges Schneiderman, five reels, presumed lost.
Cast: Shirley Mason (Jackie), William Scott (Mervyn) George E. Stone (Benny).

Little Miss Smiles (1922)
Crew: *Director* Jack Ford, ***Screenplay*** Dorothy Yost, ***Story*** Myra Kelly, ***Photography*** David Abel, five reels, presumed lost.
Cast: Shirley Mason (Esther), Gaston Glass (Dr. Jack Washton), George Williams (Papa Aaronson).

Silver Wings (1922)
Crew: *Director*s Edwin Carewe, Jack Ford (prologue), ***Screenplay*** Paul Sloane, ***Photography*** Joseph Ruttenberg, Robert Kurrle, 8,271 feet, presumed lost.
Cast: Mary Carr (Anna), Lynn Hammond (John).

The Village Blacksmith (1922)
Crew: *Director* Jack Ford, ***Screenplay*** Paul H. Sloane, ***Poem*** Henry Wadsworth Longfellow, ***Photography*** George Schneiderman, eight reels, one reel exists.
Cast: William Walling (John Hammond), David Butler (Bill), Virginia Valli (Alice Hammond).

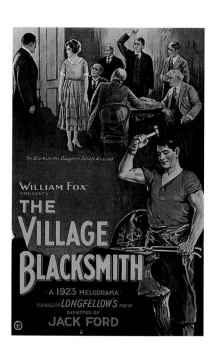

The Face on the Barroom Floor
(The Love Image, 1923)
Crew: *Director* Jack Ford, *Screenplay* Eugene B.
Lewis, G. Marion Burton, *Poem* Hugh Antoine
D'Arcy, *Photography* George Schneiderman,
5,787 feet, presumed lost.
Cast: Henry B. Walthall (Stevens), Ruth Clifford
(Marion), Walter Emerson (Von Vleck).

Three Jumps Ahead *(1923)*
Crew: *Director/Screenplay* Jack Ford,
Photography Daniel Clark, 4,854 feet, presumed
lost.
Cast: Tom Mix (Steve), Alma Bennett (Annie),
Edward Peil (Taggitt).

Cameo Kirby *(1923)*
Crew: *Director* John Ford, *Screenplay* Robert N.
Lee, *Play* Harry Leon Wilson, Booth Tarkington,
Photography George Schneiderman, 7 reels.
Cast: John Gilbert (Kirby), Gertrude Olmstead
(Adele), Alan Hale (Moreau).

North of Hudson Bay *(North of the Yukon, 1923)*
Crew: *Director* John Ford, *Screenplay* Jules
Furthman, *Photography* Daniel Clark, five reels,
40 minutes exists.
Cast: Tom Mix (Dane), Kathleen Key (Estelle),
Frank Campeau (MacDonald).

Hoodman Blind *(1923)*
Crew: *Director* John Ford, *Screenplay* Charles
Kenyon, *Play* Henry Arthur Jones, Wilson Barrett,
Photography George Schneiderman, 5,434 feet,
presumed lost.
Cast: David Butler (Jack), Gladys Hulette (Nancy),
Frank Campeau (Lezzard).

The Iron Horse *(1924)*
Crew: *Director* John Ford, *Screenplay* Charles
Kenyon, *Story* Kenyon, John Russell,
Photography George Schneiderman, Burnett
Guffey, 11, 335 feet.
Cast: George O'Brien (Davy Brandon), Madge
Bellamy (Miriam), Fred Kohler (Deroux), J. Farrell
MacDonald (Corporal Casey).

Hearts of Oak *(1924)*
Crew: *Director* John Ford, *Screenplay* Charles
Kenyon, *Play* James Herne, *Photography* George
Schneiderman, 5,336 feet, presumed lost.
Cast: Hobart Bosworth (Dunnivan), Pauline Starke
(Chrystal), Theodore von Eltz (Ned Fairweather).

Lightnin' *(1925)*
Crew: *Director* John Ford, *Screenplay* Frances
Marion, *Play* Winchell Smith, Frank Bacon,
Photography Joe August, 8,050 feet.
Cast: Jay Hunt (Lightnin' Bill Jones), Madge
Bellamy (Millie), Wallace McDonald (Marvin).

Kentucky Pride *(1925)*
Crew: *Director* John Ford, *Screenplay* Dorothy
Yost, *Photography* George Schneiderman, 6,597
feet.
Cast: Henry B. Walthall (Mr Beaumont), J. Farrell
MacDonald (Mike Donovan), Gertrude Astor (Mrs
Beaumont).

The Fighting Heart *(1925)*
Crew: *Director* John Ford, *Screenplay* Lillie
Hayward, *Story* Larry Evans, *Photography* Joe
August, 6,978 feet, presumed lost.
Cast: George O'Brien (Bolton), Billie Dove (Doris),
J. Farrell MacDonald (Jerry), Victor McLaglen
(Soapy).

Thank You *(1925)*
Crew: *Director* John Ford, *Screenplay* Frances
Marion, *Play* Winchell Smith, Tom Cushing,
Photography George Schneiderman, 75 minutes,
presumed lost.
Cast: George O'Brien (Jamieson), Jacqueline Logan
(Diane), Alec Francis (David).

The Shamrock Handicap *(1926)*
Crew: *Director* John Ford, *Screenplay* John
Stone, *Story* Peter B. Kyne, *Photography* George
Schneiderman, 5,685 feet.
Cast: Janet Gaynor (Sheila), Leslie Fenton (Neil), J.
Farrell MacDonald (O'Shea).

3 Bad Men *(1926)*
Crew: *Director* John Ford, *Screenplay* Ford, John
Stone, *Novel* Herman Whitaker, *Photography*
George Schneiderman, 8,710 feet.
Cast: George O'Brien (O'Malley), J. Farrell
MacDonald (Mike), Tom Santschi (Bull).

The Blue Eagle *(1926)*
Crew: *Director* John Ford, *Screenplay* L. G.
Rigby, *Story* Gerald Beaumont, *Photography*
George Schneiderman, 6,200 feet, sea battle
sequence missing.
Cast: George O'Brien (Darcy), Janet Gaynor
(Rose), William Russell (Tim).

Upstream *(1927)*
Crew: *Director* John Ford, *Screenplay* Randall
Faye, *Story* Wallace Smith, *Photography* Charles
G. Clarke, 5,510 feet, presumed lost.
Cast: Nancy Nash (Gertie), Earle Foxe
(Brasingham), Grant Withers (Jack).

Mother Machree *(1928)*
Crew: *Director* John Ford, *Screenplay* Gertrude
Orr, *Story* Rida Johnson Young, *Photography*
Chester Lyons, 75 minutes, three reels exist.
Cast: Belle Bennett (Ellen McHugh), Neil
Hamilton (Brian), Victor McLaglen (Terence).

Four Sons *(1928)*
Crew: *Director* John Ford, *Screenplay* Philip
Klein, *Story* I. A. R. Wylie, *Photography* George
Schneiderman, Charles G. Clarke, 100 minutes.
Cast: Margaret Mann (Frau Bernle), James Hall
(Joseph), Charles Morton (Johann).

Hangman's House *(1928)*
Crew: *Director* John Ford, *Screenplay* Marion
Orth, Willard Mack, *Novel* Donn Byrne,
Photography George Schneiderman, 75 minutes.
Cast: Victor McLaglen (Hogan), June Collyer
(Connaught), Earle Foxe (D'Arcy).

THE BLACK WATCH

WILLIAM FOX
ALL TALKING FOX MOVIETONE FEATURE
VICTOR M. LAGLEN
MYRNA LOY · DAVID ROLLINS · ROY D'ARCY
directed by JOHN FORD

Napoleon's Barber *(1928)*

Crew: *Director* John Ford, *Screenplay/Play* Arthur Caesar, *Photography* George Schneiderman, 32 minutes, presumed lost.
Cast: Otto Matieson (Napoleon), Frank Reicher (Barber).

Riley the Cop *(1928)*

Crew: *Director* John Ford, *Screenplay* James Gruen, Fred Stanley, *Photography* Charles G. Clarke, 67 minutes.
Cast: J. Farrell MacDonald (Riley), Louise Fazenda (Lena), David Rollins (Davy).

Strong Boy *(1929)*

Crew: *Director* John Ford, *Screenplay* James Kevin McGuinness, Andrew Bennison, John McLain, *Story* Frederick Hazlitt Brennan, *Photography* Joseph August, 63 minutes, presumed lost (an Australian print is rumoured).
Cast: Victor McLaglen (Strong Boy), Leatrice Joy (Mary), Clyde Cook (Pete).

The Black Watch *(1929)*

Crew: *Director* John Ford, *Screenplay* James Kevin McGuinness, John Stone, *Novel* Talbot Mundy, *Photography* Joe August, 93 minutes.
Cast: Victor McLaglen (King), Myrna Loy (Yasmani) Walter Long (Harem Bey).

Salute *(1929)*

Crew: *Director* John Ford, *Screenplay* James Kevin McGuinness, *Story* Tristram Tupper, John Stone, *Photography* Joe August, 86 minutes.
Cast: George O'Brien (Randall), Helen Chandler (Nancy), Stepin Fetchit (Smoke Screen), Ward Bond, John Wayne (Football players).

Men Without Women *(1930)*

Crew: *Director* John Ford, *Screenplay*, Dudley Nichols, *Story* Ford, James Kevin McGuinness, *Photography* Joe August, 77 minutes.
Cast: Kenneth MacKenna (Burke), Frank Albertson (Price), Stuart Erwin (Jenkins).

Born Reckless *(1930)*

Crew: *Director* John Ford, *Screenplay* Dudley Nichols, *Novel* Donald Henderson Clarke, *Photography* George Schneiderman, 82 minutes.
Cast: Edmund Lowe (Beretti), Catherine Dale Owen (Joan), Lee Tracy (O'Brien).

Up The River *(1930)*

Crew: *Director* John Ford, *Screenplay* Maurine Watkins, *Photography* Joe August, 92 minutes.
Cast: Spencer Tracy (St. Louis), Warren Hymer (Dannemora Dan), Humphrey Bogart (Steve).

Seas Beneath *(1931)*

Crew: *Director* John Ford, *Screenplay* Dudley Nichols, *Story* James Parker, Jr., *Photography* Joe August, 99 minutes.
Cast: George O'Brien (Commander Kingsley), Marion Lessing (Anna Von Steuben), Warren Hymer (Kaufman).

The Brat *(1931)*

Crew: *Director* John Ford, *Screenplay* Sonya Levien, S. N. Behrman, Maude Fulton, *Play* Fulton, *Photography* Joe August, 81 minutes.
Cast: Sally O'Neill (The Brat), Alan Dinehart (M. Forester), Frank Albertson (S. Forester).

Arrowsmith *(1931)*

Crew: *Director* John Ford, *Screenplay* Sidney Howard, *Novel* Sinclair Lewis, *Photography* Ray June, 108 minutes.
Cast: Ronald Colman (Arrowsmith), Helen Hayes (Leora), Myrna Loy (Joyce).

Air Mail *(1932)*

Crew: *Director* John Ford, *Screenplay* Dale Van Every, Frank Wead, *Story* Wead, *Photography* Karl Freund, 83 minutes.
Cast: Pat O'Brien (Talbot), Ralph Bellamy (Miller), Gloria Stuart (Ruth Barnes).

Flesh *(1932)*

Crew: *Director* John Ford, *Screenplay* Leonard Praskins, Edgar Allen Woolf, *Story* Edmund Goulding, *Photography* Arthur Edeson, 95 minutes.
Cast: Wallace Beery (Polakai), Karen Morley (Lora), Ricardo Cortez (Nicky).

Pilgrimage *(1933)*

Crew: *Director* John Ford, *Screenplay* Philip Klein, Barry Connors, *Dialogue* Dudley Nichols, *Story* I. A. L Wylie, *Photography* George Schneiderman, 90 minutes.
Cast: Henrietta Crosman (Hannah), Heather Angel (Suzanne), Norman Foster (Jim).

Doctor Bull *(1933)*

Crew: *Director* John Ford, *Screenplay* Paul Green, *Novel* James Gould Cozzens, *Photography* George Schneiderman, 76 minutes.
Cast: Will Rogers (Bull), Marian Nixon (May), Berton Churchill (Banning).

The Lost Patrol *(1934)*

Crew: *Director* John Ford, *Screenplay* Dudley Nichols, Garret Fort, *Story* Philip MacDonald, *Photography* Harold Wenstrom, 74 minutes.
Cast: Victor McLaglen (Sergeant), Boris Karloff (Sanders), Wallace Ford (Morelli).

The World Moves On *(1934)*

Crew: *Director* John Ford, *Screenplay* Reginald C. Berkeley, *Photography* George Schneiderman, 90 minutes.
Cast: Franchot Tone (Girard), Madeleine Carroll (Mrs Warburton), Reginald Denny (Von Gerhardt).

Judge Priest *(1934)*

Crew: *Director* John Ford, *Screenplay* Dudley Nichols, Lamar Trotti, *Stories* Irvin S. Cobb, *Photography* George Schneiderman, 80 minutes.
Cast: Will Rogers (Priest), Henry B. Walthall (Rev. Brand), Anita Louise (Ellie May Gillespie).

The Whole Town's Talking *(1935)*

Crew: *Director* John Ford, *Screenplay* Jo Swerling, *Novel* W. R. Burnett, *Photography* Joseph Walker, 95 minutes.
Cast: Edward G. Robinson (Jones/Mannion), Jean Arthur (Miss Bill Jones) Wallace Ford (Healy).

The Informer (1935)

Crew: *Director* John Ford, *Screenplay* Dudley Nichols, *Novel* Liam O'Flaherty, *Photography* Joe August, 91 minutes.
Cast: Victor McLaglen (Nolan), Heather Angel (Mary McPhilip), Preston Foster (Gallagher).

Steamboat Round the Bend (1935)

Crew: *Director* John Ford, *Screenplay* Dudley Nichols, Lamar Trotti, *Story* Ben Lucian Burman, *Photography* George Schneiderman, 80 minutes.
Cast: Will Rogers (Pearly), Anne Shirley (Fleety Belle), Berton Churchill (The New Moses), Stepin Fetchit (Jonah).

The Prisoner of Shark Island (1936)

Crew: *Director* John Ford, *Screenplay* Nunnally Johnson, *Photography* Bert Glennon, 95 minutes.
Cast: Warner Baxter (Mudd), Gloria Stuart (Peggy Mudd), Harry Carey (Commandant), John Carradine (Rankin).

Mary of Scotland (1936)

Crew: *Director* John Ford, *Screenplay* Dudley Nichols, *Play* Maxwell Anderson, *Photography* Joe August, 123 minutes.
Cast: Katharine Hepburn (Mary Stuart), Fredric March (Bothwell), Florence Eldridge (Elizabeth I.).

The Plough and the Stars (1936)

Crew: *Director* John Ford, *Screenplay* Dudley Nichols, *Play* Sean O'Casey, *Photography* Joe August, 67 minutes.
Cast: Barbara Stanwyck (Nora Clitheroe), Preston Foster (Clitheroe), Barry Fitzgerald (Good).

Wee Willie Winkie (1937)

Crew: *Director* John Ford, *Screenplay* Ernest Pascal, Julian Josephson, *Story* Rudyard Kipling, *Photography* Arthur Miller, 99 minutes.
Cast: Shirley Temple (Priscilla), Victor McLaglen (MacDuff), C. Aubrey Smith (Williams), Cesar Romero (Khoda Khan).

The Hurricane (1937)

Crew: *Director* John Ford, *Screenplay* Dudley Nichols, *Novel* Charles Nordhoff, James Norman Hall, *Photography* Bert Glennon, 102 minutes.
Cast: Dorothy Lamour (Marama), Jon Hall (Terangi), Mary Astor (Mrs DeLaage), C. Aubrey Smith (Father Paul).

Four Men and a Prayer (1938)

Crew: *Director* John Ford, *Screenplay* Richard Sherman, Sonya Levien, Walter Ferris, *Novel* David Garth, *Photography* Ernest Palmer, 85 minutes.
Cast: Loretta Young (Lynn Cherrington), Richard Greene (Geoff Leigh), George Sanders (Wyatt Leigh), David Niven (Chris Leigh), William Henry (Rodney Leigh).

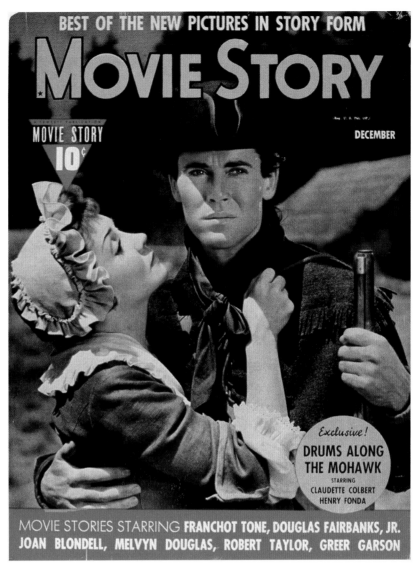

Submarine Patrol (1938)

Crew: *Director* John Ford, *Screenplay* Rian James, Darrell Ware, Jack Yellen, *Novel* John Milholland, *Photography* Arthur Miller, 95 minutes.
Cast: Richard Greene (Townsend) Nancy Kelly (Susan Leeds), Preston Foster (Drake).

Stagecoach (1939)

Crew: *Director*/Producer: John Ford, *Screenplay* Dudley Nichols, *Story* Ernest Haycox, *Photography* Bert Glennon, 97 minutes.
Cast: John Wayne (Ringo), Claire Trevor (Dallas), John Carradine (Hatfield), Thomas Mitchell (Dr. Boone).

Young Mr. Lincoln (1939)

Crew: *Director* John Ford, *Screenplay* Lamar Trotti, *Photography* Bert Glennon, 101 minutes.

Cast: Henry Fonda (Lincoln), Alice Brady (Mrs Clay), Ward Bond (Cass), Milburn Stone (Douglas).

Drums Along the Mohawk (1939)

Crew: *Director* John Ford, *Screenplay* Lamar Trotti, Sonya Levien, *Novel* Walter D. Edmonds, *Photography* Bert Glennon, Ray Rennahan, Colour, 103 minutes.
Cast: Henry Fonda (Martin), Claudette Colbert (Mrs Martin), Edna May Oliver (Mrs McKlennan), John Carradine (Caldwell).

The Grapes of Wrath (1940)

Crew: *Director* John Ford, *Screenplay* Nunnally Johnson, *Novel* John Steinbeck, *Photography* Gregg Toland, 129 minutes.
Cast: Henry Fonda (Joad), Jane Darwell (Ma Joad), John Carradine (Casey), Charley Grapewin (Grampa).

The Long Voyage Home (1940)
Crew: *Director* John Ford, *Screenplay*, Dudley Nichols, *Plays* Eugene O'Neill, *Photography* Gregg Toland, 105 minutes.
Cast: John Wayne (Ole), Thomas Mitchell (Driscoll), Barry Fitzgerald (Cocky), Ward Bond (Yank).

Tobacco Road (1941)
Crew: *Director* John Ford, *Screenplay* Nunnally Johnson, *Play* Jack Kirkland, *Novel* Erskine Caldwell, *Photography* Arthur Miller, 84 minutes.
Cast: Charley Grapewin (Jeeter Lester), Marjorie Rambeau (Bessie), Gene Tierney (Ellie May Lester), Dana Andrews (Captain Tim).

How Green Was My Valley (1941)
Crew: *Director* John Ford, *Screenplay* Philip Dunne, *Novel* Richard Llewellyn, *Photography* Arthur Miller, 118 minutes.
Cast: Walter Pidgeon (Mr Gruffydd), Maureen O'Hara (Angharad), Donald Crisp (Mr Morgan), Roddy McDowall (Huw).

The Battle of Midway (1942)
Crew: *Director* Lt. Commander John Ford, U.S.N.R. *Narration written by* John Ford, Dudley Nichols, James Kevin McGuinness, *Photography* John Ford, Jack McKenzie, 20 minutes.
Cast: Voices of Henry Fonda, Jane Darwell, Donald Crisp, Irving Pichel.

December 7th (1943)
Crew: *Director*s Lt. Gregg Toland, U.S.N.R., Lt. Commander John Ford, U.S.N.R, *Photography* Gregg Toland, 34 minutes.

They Were Expendable (1945)
Crew: *Director/Producer* John Ford, *Screenplay* Frank W. Wead, *Book* William L. White, *Photography* Joseph August, 136 minutes.
Cast: Robert Montgomery (Lt. John Brickley), John Wayne (Lt. Rusty Ryan), Donna Reed (Lt. Sandy Davis), Jack Holt (Gen. Martin), Ward Bond (Boats Mulcahey).

My Darling Clementine (1946)
Crew: *Director* John Ford, *Screenplay* Winston Miller, Samuel G. Engel, *Book Wyatt Earp, Frontier Marshall* Stuart Lake, *Photography* Joseph MacDonald, 97 minutes.
Cast: Henry Fonda (Wyatt Earp), Victor Mature (Doc Holliday), Walter Brennan (Old Man Clanton).

The Fugitive (1947)
Crew: *Director* John Ford, *Screenplay* Dudley Nichols, *Novel The Power and the Glory* Graham Greene, *Photography* Gabriel Figueroa, 104 minutes.
Cast: Henry Fonda (The Fugitive), Dolores del Rio (Mexican Woman), Pedro Armandáriz (Lieutenant), Ward Bond (El Gringo).

Fort Apache (1948)
Crew: *Director* John Ford, *Screenplay* Frank S. Nugent, *Story* James Warner Bellah, *Photography* Archie Stout, William Clothier, 127 minutes.
Cast: John Wayne (Kirby York), Henry Fonda (Thursday), Shirley Temple (Philadelphia Thursday), Ward Bond (O'Rourke).

3 Godfathers (1948)
Crew: *Director* John Ford, *Screenplay* Laurence Stallings, Frank S. Nugent, *Story* Peter B. Kyne, *Photography* Winton C. Hoch, Colour, 106 minutes.
Cast: John Wayne (Hightower), Pedro Armandáriz (Fuerte), Harry Carey, Jr. (Kearney), Ward Bond (Sweet).

She Wore a Yellow Ribbon (1949)
Crew: *Director* John Ford, *Screenplay* Frank S. Nugent, Laurence Stallings, *Story* James Warner Bellah, *Photography* Winton S. Hoch, Colour, 103 minutes.
Cast: John Wayne (Brittles), Joanne Dru (Olivia), Victor McLaglen (Quincannon), Ben Johnson (Tyree), Harry Carey, Jr. (Pennell).

When Willie Comes Marching Home (1950)
Crew: *Director* John Ford, *Screenplay* Mary Loos, Richard Sale, *Story* Sy Gomberg, *Photography* Leo Tover, 82 minutes.
Cast: Dan Dailey (Kluggs), Corinne Calvet (Yvonne), William Demarest (Herman Kluggs).

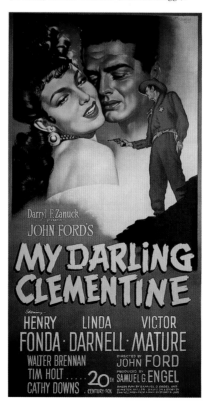

Wagon Master (1950)
Crew: *Director* John Ford, *Screenplay* Frank S. Nugent, Patrick Ford, *Photography* Bert Glennon, Archie Stout, 86 minutes.
Cast: Ben Johnson (Blue), Harry Carey, Jr. (Owens), Ward Bond (Wiggs), Joanne Dru (Denver).

Rio Grande (1950)
Crew: *Director* John Ford, *Screenplay* James Kevin McGuinness, *Story* James Warner Bellah, *Photography* Bert Glennon, Archie Stout, 105 minutes.
Cast: John Wayne (York), Maureen O'Hara (Mrs York), Ben Johnson (Tyree), Claude Jarman, Jr. (Trooper York).

This Is Korea! (1951)
Crew: *Director* Rear Admiral John Ford U.S.N.R., 50 minutes.
Cast: Voices of John Ireland and others.

The Quiet Man (1952)
Crew: *Director* John Ford, *Screenplay* Frank S. Nugent, *Story* Maurice Walsh, *Photography* Winton C. Hoch, Archie Stout, Colour, 129 minutes.
Cast: John Wayne (Thornton), Maureen O'Hara (Danaher), Victor McLaglen (Red Will Danaher), Ward Bond (Father Lonergan).

What Price Glory (1952)
Crew: *Director* John Ford, *Screenplay* Phoebe and Henry Ephron, *Play* Maxwell Anderson, Laurence Stallings, *Photography* Joseph MacDonald, Colour, 111 minutes.
Cast: James Cagney (Flagg), Dan Dailey (Quirt), Corinne Calvet (Charmaine), William Demarest (Kiper).

The Sun Shines Bright (1953)
Crew: *Director* John Ford, *Screenplay* Laurence Stallings, *Stories* Irvin S. Cobb, *Photography* Archie Stout, 90 minutes.
Cast: Charles Winninger (Judge Priest), Stepin Fetchit (Poindexter), Arleen Whelan (Lucy Lee Lake).

Mogambo (1953)
Crew: *Director* John Ford, *Screenplay* John Lee Mahin, *Play* Wilson Collison, *Photography* Robert Surtees, Freddie Young, Colour, 116 minutes.
Cast: Clark Gable (Marswell), Grace Kelly (Nordley), Ava Gardner (Kelly).

The Long Gray Line (1955)
Crew: *Director* John Ford, *Screenplay* Edward Hope, *Book* Marty Maher, Nardi Reeder Campion, *Photography* Charles Lawton, Jr., Colour, 138 minutes.
Cast: Tyrone Power (Maher), Maureen O'Hara (Mary O'Donnell), Robert Francis (Sundstrom).

The Red, White and Blue Line
(1955)
Crew: *Director* John Ford, *Screenplay* Edward Hope, *Photography* Charles Lawton, Jr., 10 minutes.
Cast: Narrator Ward Bond.

Mister Roberts *(1955)*
Crew: *Director*s John Ford, Mervyn LeRoy, *Screenplay* Frank S. Nugent, Joshua Logan, *Play* Logan, Thomas Heggen, *Novel* Heggen, *Photography* Winton C. Hoch, Colour, 123 minutes.
Cast: Henry Fonda (Roberts), James Cagney (Captain), Jack Lemmon (Pulver).

The Bamboo Cross *(1955)*
Episode of the *Fireside Theater* TV series.
Crew: *Director* John Ford, *Screenplay* Laurence Stallings, *Play* Theophane Lee, *Photography* John McBurnie, 27 minutes.
Cast: Jane Wyman (Sister Regina).

Rookie of the Year *(1955)*
Episode of the *Screen Director's Playhouse* TV series.
Crew: *Director* John Ford, 29 minutes.
Cast: Pat Wayne (Lyn Goodhue), Vera Miles (Rose Goodhue), Ward Bond (Larry Goodhue), John Wayne (Mike Cronin, a reporter).

The Searchers *(1956)*
Crew: *Director* John Ford, *Screenplay* Frank S. Nugent, *Novel* Alan LeMay, *Photography* Winton C. Hoch, Alfred Gilks, Colour, 119 minutes.
Cast: John Wayne (Ethan Edwards), Jeffrey Hunter (Pawley), Vera Miles (Jorgenson), Ward Bond (Clayton).

The Rising of the Moon *(1957)*
Crew: *Director* John Ford, *Screenplay* Frank S. Nugent, *Story* Frank O'Connor, *Plays* Michael McHugh, Lady Gregory, *Photography* Robert Krasker, 81 minutes.
Cast: Tyrone Power (Narrator), Cyril Cusack (Dillon), Donal Donnelly (Curran).

The Wings of Eagles *(1957)*
Crew: *Director* John Ford, *Screenplay* Frank Fenton, William Wister Haines, *Photography* Paul C. Vogel, Colour, 110 minutes.
Cast: John Wayne (Wead), Maureen O'Hara (Mrs Wead), Dan Dailey (Carson), Ward Bond (John Dodge).

The Last Hurrah *(1958)*
Crew: *Director/Producer* John Ford, *Screenplay* Frank S. Nugent, *Novel* Edwin O'Connor, *Photography* Charles Lawton, Jr., 121 minutes.
Cast: Spencer Tracy (Skeffington), Jeffrey Hunter (Caulfield), Pat O'Brien (Gorman), Basil Rathbone (Cass).

Gideon of Scotland Yard
(Gideon's Day, 1958)
Crew: *Director* John Ford, *Screenplay* T.E.B. Clarke, *Novel* J.J. Marric, *Photography* Freddie Young, Colour, 91 minutes.
Cast: Jack Hawkins (Gideon), Dianne Foster (Delafield), Cyril Cusack (Sparrow).

Korea: Battleground for Liberty
(1959)
Crew: *Director* Rear Admiral John Ford, USNR, 40 minutes.
Cast: George O'Brien, Kim-Chi Mi, Choi My Ryonk.

The Horse Soldiers *(1959)*
Crew: *Director* John Ford, *Screenplay* John Lee Mahin, Martin Rackin, *Novel* Harold Sinclair, *Photography* William L. Clothier, Colour, 119 minutes.
Cast: John Wayne (Marlowe), William Holden (Kendall), Constance Towers (Hannah Hunter), Althea Gibson (Lukey).

The Colter Craven Story *(1960)*
Episode of the *Wagon Train* TV series.
Crew: *Director* John Ford, *Screenplay* Tony Paulson, *Photography* Ben Kline, 53 minutes.

Cast: Ward Bond (Seth Adams), Carleton Young (Craven), John Carradine (Park), Marion Michael Morrison, i.e. John Wayne (Gen. Sherman).

Sergeant Rutledge *(1960)*

Crew: *Director* John Ford, *Screenplay* Willis Goldbeck, James Warner Bellah, *Photography* Bert Glennon, Colour, 111 minutes.
Cast: Jeffrey Hunter (Cantrell), Woody Strode (Rutledge), Constance Towers (Mary Beecher), Juano Hernandez (Skimore).

The Alamo *(1960)*

Crew: *Director* John Wayne, John Ford (uncredited second unit), *Screenplay* James Edward Grant, *Photography* William Clothier, Colour, 190 minutes.
Cast: John Wayne (Crockett), Richard Widmark (Bowie), Laurence Harvey (Travis).

Two Rode Together *(1961)*

Crew: *Director* John Ford, *Screenplay* Frank S. Nugent, *Novel* Will Cook, *Photography* Charles Lawton, Jr., Colour, 109 minutes.
Cast: James Stewart (McCabe), Richard Widmark (Gary), Shirley Jones (Purcell).

The Man Who Shot Liberty Valance *(1962)*

Crew: *Director* John Ford, *Screenplay* Willis Goldbeck, James Warner Bellah, *Story* Dorothy B. Johnson, *Photography* William H. Clothier, 122 minutes.
Cast: John Wayne (Doniphon), James Stewart (Stoddard), Lee Marvin (Valance), Vera Miles (Hallie Stoddard).

Flashing Spikes *(1962)*

Crew: *Director* John Ford, *Screenplay* Jameson Brewer, *Novel* Frank O'Rourke, *Photography* William H. Clothier, 53 minutes.
Cast: James Stewart (Slim), Jack Warden (Commissioner), Pat Wayne (Bill).

How the West Was Won *(1962)*

Crew: *Directors* John Ford (The Civil War), George Marshall (The Railroad), Henry Hathaway (The Rivers, The Plains, The Outlaws), *Screenplay* James R. Webb, based on a series in *Life* magazine, *Photography* Joseph LaShelle, Colour, 162 minutes.
Cast: John Wayne (Sherman), Harry Morgan (Grant), George Peppard (Rawlings).

Donovan's Reef *(1963)*

Crew: *Director/Producer* John Ford, *Screenplay* Frank Nugent, James Edward Grant, *Story* Edmund Beloin, *Adaptation* James Michener, *Photography* William H. Clothier, Colour, 109 minutes.
Cast: John Wayne (Donovan), Lee Marvin (Gilhooley), Elizabeth Allen (Sarah Dedham).

Cheyenne Autumn *(1964)*

Crew: *Director* John Ford, *Screenplay* James R. Webb, *Book* Mari Sandoz, *Photography* William H. Clothier, Colour, 159 minutes.
Cast: Richard Widmark (Archer), Carroll Baker (Deborah Wright), James Stewart (Wyatt Earp).

Young Cassidy *(1965)*

Crew: *Directors* Jack Cardiff, John Ford, *Screenplay* John Whiting, *Autobiography* Sean O'Casey, *Photography* Ted Scaife, Colour, 110 minutes.
Cast: Rod Taylor (Cassidy), Maggie Smith (Nora), Julie Christie (Daisy Battles).

7 Women *(1966)*

Crew: *Director* John Ford, *Screenplay* Janet Green, John McCormick, *Story* Norah Lofts, *Photography* Joseph LaShelle, Colour, 87 minutes.
Cast: Anne Bancroft (Cartwright), Sue Lyon (Emma Clark), Margaret Leighton (Andrews).

Chesty: A Tribute to a Legend *(1976)*

Crew: *Director* John Ford, *Writer* Jay Simms, *Photography* Brick Marquard, Colour, 87 minutes.
Cast: John Wayne (Host), Lieutenant General Lewis "Chesty" Puller, USMC.

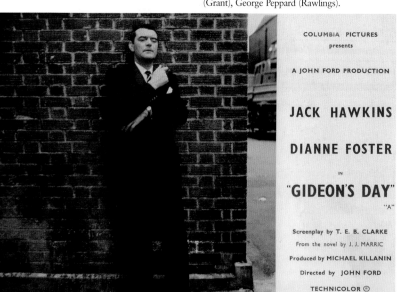

Bibliography

Biographies
– Eyman, Scott: *Print the Legend: The Life and Times of John Ford.* Simon & Shuster 1999
– Ford, Dan: *Pappy: The Life of John Ford.* Prentice-Hall 1979
– McBride, Joseph: *Searching for John Ford.* St Martin's 2001
– Sinclair, Andrew: *John Ford.* Dial 1979

Analysis, Memoirs
– Anderson, Lindsay: *About John Ford.* McGraw-Hill 1981
– Baxter, John: *The Cinema of John Ford.* A. S. Barnes 1971
– Bogdanovich, Peter: *John Ford.* University of California Press 1994
– Carey Jr., Harry: *Company of Heroes.* Scarecrow Press 1994
– Darby, William: *John Ford's Westerns.* McFarland 1996
– Davis, Ronald L.: *John Ford: Hollywood's Old Master.* University of Oklahoma Press 1995
– Gallagher, Tag: *John Ford: The Man and His Films.* University of California Press 1986
– McBride, Joseph & Wilmington, Michael: *John Ford.* De Capo 1975
– Mitry, Jean: *John Ford.* Editions Universitaires 1964
– Place, J. A.: *The Non-Western Films of John Ford.* Citadel 1979
– Place, J.A.: *The Western Films of John Ford.* Citadel 1974
– Sarris, Andrew: *The John Ford Movie Mystery.* Indiana University Press 1975

On Specific Films
– Buscombe, Edward: *Stagecoach.* BFI 1992
– Dunne, Philip: *How Green Was My Valley: The Screenplay.* Santa Teresa Press 1996
– McNee, Gerry: *In the Footsteps of The Quiet Man.* Mainstream Publishing 1990

Background
– Behlmer, Rudy: *Memo from Darryl F. Zanuck.* Grove Press 1993
– Eyman, Scott: *The Speed of Sound.* Simon & Shuster 1997
– Fenin, George N. & Everson, William K.: *The Western: From Silents to the Seventies.* Grossman 1973
– Parrish, Robert: *Growing Up in Hollywood.* Harecourt Brace Jovanovich 1976
– Roberts, Randy & Olson, James S.: *John Wayne, American.* Free Press 1995
– Silver, Charles: *The Western Film.* Pyramid 1976
– Tuska, Jon: *The Filming of the West.* Doubleday 1976
– Wurtzel Semenov, Lillian & Winter, Carla: *William Fox, Sol M. Wurtzel and the Early Fox Film Corporation, Letters 1917–1923.* McFarland 2001

Documentaries
– *Directed by John Ford* (1971) Director/Screenplay Peter Bogdanovich, narrator Orson Welles, with John Ford, 95 minutes.
– *The American West of John Ford* (1971), Director Denis Sanders, with John Ford, John Wayne, James Stewart, Henry Fonda, 58 minutes.
– *The American Film Institute First Annual Life Achievement Award* (1973) Director Robert Scheerer, with John Ford, John Wayne, Maureen O'Hara, Danny Kaye, President Richard Nixon, 75 minutes.

Websites
– www.imdb.com
– www.sensesofcinema.com

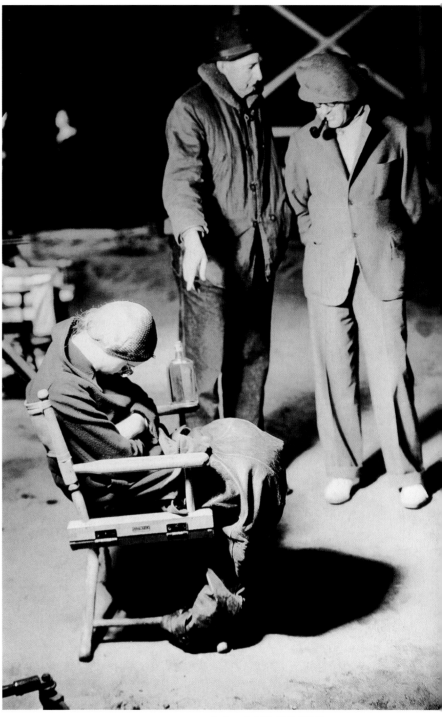

On the set of 'Air Mail' (1932)
An example of John Ford's humour. Gloria Stuart fell asleep during the night shoot so John Ford placed a whiskey bottle beside her, posed Slim Summerville and had this photo taken.

Playing Cards

If John Ford phoned to invite you to a card game, then you dropped what you were doing and went running. Even if you were John Wayne (left), Henry Fonda (centre) or Ward Bond (right). Ford always won. However, if one of the stuntmen or actors lost a lot of money and couldn't afford it, then Ford surreptitiously arranged for them to get extra work, or to be required on set throughout the shoot whether or not they were needed.